Understanding
the
HOLOCAUST

Understanding the HOLOCAUST

VOLUME 2

GEORGE FELDMAN

DETROIT • LONDON

Understanding the
HOLOCAUST

by George Feldman

Staff

Julie L. Carnagie, *U·X·L Developmental Editor*
Sonia Benson, Senior *U·X·L Developmental Editor*
Carol DeKane Nagel, *U·X·L Managing Editor*
Thomas L. Romig, *U·X·L Publisher*

Mary Beth Trimper, *Production Director*
Evi Seoud, *Production Manager*
Shanna P. Heilveil, *Production Associate*

Cynthia Baldwin, *Product Design Manager*
Barbara J. Yarrow, *Graphic Services Supervisor*
Tracey Rowens, *Art Director*

Margaret A. Chamberlain, *Permissions Specialist*

Library of Congress Cataloging-in-Publication Data

Feldman, George.
    Understanding the Holocaust / Feorge Feldman
        p.   cm.
    Includes bibliographical references and index.
    ISBN 0-7876-1740-7 (set). — 0-7876-1741-5 (v. 1.) — 0-7876-1742-3 (v. 2)
    1. Holocaust, Jewish (1939-1945)--Causes. 2. Germany—Politics and government—1933-1945. 3. Germany—History—1933-1945. 4. National socialism.   I. Title.

    D804.3.F46 1998
    940.53'18—dc21

                             97-26864
                             CIP AC

Printed in the United States of America
10 9 8 7 6 5 4 3 2

To my father, Benjamin, who fought in the French Army against the Nazis and escaped to hide,

To my mother, Sonia, who lived in hiding in Limoges,

To my sister, Renée, who was born in hiding, and who looks, in old pictures, like the children who disappeared,

To my uncle Boris, who fought in the French Army against the Nazis, was captured, and spent five years as a prisoner of war,

To my aunt Lisa, his wife, who was arrested by the French police and sent to Bergen-Belsen, and came back,

To their sons, my cousins Toli and Mara, who went with her and came back,

And to my daughter, Nina, who will never have to go.

"And you shall not oppress an outsider, for you know the heart of an outsider because you were outsiders in the land of Egypt."

Exodus, Ch. 23, 9.

Contents

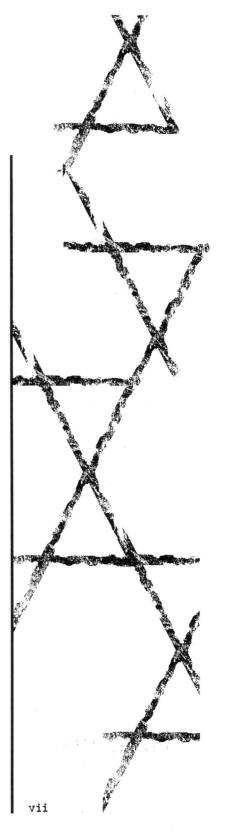

Volume 1

Volume 2

Advisory Board

S pecial thanks are due for the invaluable comments and suggestions provided by U•X•L's Holocaust Reference Library advisors:

Jonathan Betz-Zall, Children's Librarian, Sno-Isle Regional Library Systems, Edmonds, Washington

Sydney Bolkosky, Professor of History, University of Michigan-Dearborn, Dearborn, Michigan

Linda Hurwitz, Director, The Holocaust Center of Greater Pittsburgh, Pennsylvania

Debra Lyman Gniewek, Library Services Coordinator, Office of Information Technology, School District of Philadelphia, Pennsylvania

Max Weitz, Director, Holocaust Resource Center of Minneapolis, Minnesota

Reader's Guide

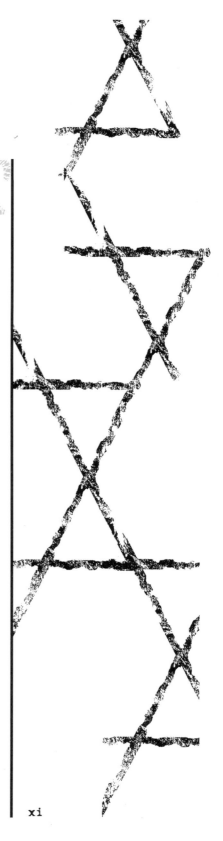

Understanding the Holocaust provides a comprehensive range of historical information and current commentary on the Holocaust, the period between 1933 and 1945 when Adolf Hitler and his Nazi Party attempted to systematically eliminate the Jews of Europe, as well as Jehovah's Witnesses, homosexuals, and other "enemies of the state." The set looks at Jewish life in Germany before the Holocaust, the economic and political conditions that gave rise to the Nazi Party, life in the ghettos where Jews were forced to live, and the horrors of the concentration and death camps. *Understanding the Holocaust* also discusses the Nuremberg trials, which saw the sentencing of some Nazi leaders for war crimes and crimes against humanity, and how the Holocaust is remembered today. These volumes describe the Holocaust in terms that help readers comprehend the events that led to it, and detail how the Nazis attempted to carry out their plan despite fighting a war on two fronts.

Understanding the Holocaust is divided into 14 chapters, each focusing on a particular topic, such as The Nazi Government and the Road to War, Auschwitz, and Life an Death in Nazi-Dominated Europe. The chapters contain numerous sidebar boxes, some focusing on people associated with the Holocaust, others taking a closer look at pivotal events. More than 120 black-and-white illustrations help to explain the text. Each volume also contains a timeline, a glossary of terms used throughout the text, an annotated bibliography of sources for further reading, and a cumulative subject index of the names, places, subjects, and terms discussed throughout *Understanding the Holocaust.*

Comments and Suggestions

We welcome your comments on *Understanding the Holocaust* and suggestions for other topics in history to consider. Please write: Editors, *Understanding the Holocaust*, U•X•L, 835 Penobscot Bldg., Detroit, Michigan 48226-4094; call toll free: 1-800-877-4253; or fax: 313-961-6347.

Author's Note:
Jewish Victims of the Holocaust by Country of Origin

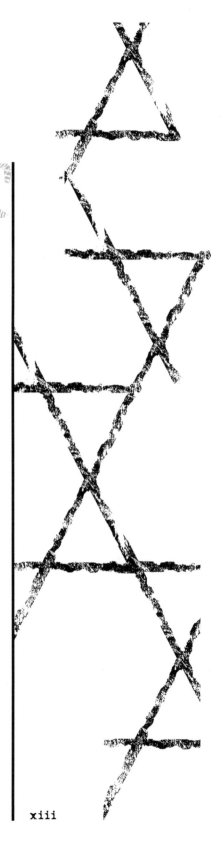

The number of Jews killed in the Holocaust is usually given as approximately 6,000,000. Although this figure was based on estimates made soon after World War II (1939–45), it has turned out to be quite accurate.

As early as April 1946, the Anglo-American Committee of Inquiry Regarding the Problems of European Jewry and Palestine reached the conclusion that 5,721,500 Jews were killed by the Nazis and their accomplices. The historian Raoul Hilberg, in his 1961 book *The Destruction of the European Jews,* gave the figures of 5,397,500 based on an estimate of the number of survivors, and of 5,100,000 based on estimates of the number of victims. Lucy S. Dawidowicz, in her 1975 book *The War Against the Jews, 1933–1945,* comes to a total of 5,933,900. In his 1982 study, *A History of the Holocaust,* Yehuda Bauer cites a figure of 5,820,960. This is very close to the total given in the chart on p. xvii, although Bauer's numbers for various countries are different than the ones used in *Understanding the Holocaust.*

There are several reasons why it is impossible to give exact figures for the number of Jews killed in the Holocaust from each country. In some countries, especially in eastern

Europe, it is not certain how many Jews there were before World War II. Many of these countries had incomplete and inaccurate records of population figures in general, not just of Jews. In addition, there is a problem in these statistics with who was considered a Jew. The Nazis defined Jews according to "race," considering anyone with Jewish ancestors to be Jewish. But Jews who had converted to Christianity, or whose parents had converted (for example in Hungary), did not consider themselves Jews. Jews who did not practice any religion (for example in urban areas of the Soviet Union) may also not have considered themselves Jews.

A second big problem with trying to determine correct figures is that statistics on the number of people killed is not accurate. Again, this is especially true in eastern Europe, specifically the Soviet Union (Russia). Relatively few Jews in western Europe were killed in their home countries. Most were arrested and deported. Because of this, there are usually records of their arrests and arrivals at transit camps, transportation by trains, and sometimes their arrivals at the place where they were killed, such as Auschwitz.

But in the Soviet Union, including areas that had been part of Poland, hundreds of thousands of people were shot within a few miles of their homes. Although the *Einsatzgruppen,* the mobile death squads that were responsible for most of these shootings, sent reports of their activities, these records are obviously not always accurate. In addition, other units—German police, army, and Waffen-SS troops, Romanian and Hungarian police and soldiers—also played a major role in these killings. So did auxiliary troops of the local population, such as in Lithuania and Ukraine. Many of the murders in the Soviet Union took place in the first weeks after the German invasion, when conditions were chaotic. It is often impossible to know, in each town, how many Jews fled eastward with the retreating Soviet army and how many stayed behind and were killed by the Nazis. Part of this difficulty can be overcome by counting survivors, rather than victims, and scholars and historians have tried to do this. This is one reason why experts now agree on the approximate number of Jews killed in the Soviet-Polish area, even though the number killed in any particular place may be uncertain.

Another example of the uncertainty of the statistics is that the figure for those killed at Auschwitz was originally estimated at around 4,000,000, while scholars now believe the number was closer to a 1,500,000. But the vast number of people killed at the Treblinka, Sobibór, and Belzec death camps was not known after the war, and the scale of shootings by the *Einsatzgruppen* was underestimated.

A third major difficulty in determining the number of victims of the Holocaust involves the many border changes that occurred in Europe from 1938 through the years of the war. Hundreds of thousands of Jews who had been Polish citizens until 1939 came under Soviet jurisdiction in that year. Many of them were killed beginning in the summer of 1941, when Germany invaded the Soviet Union. Sometimes they are counted as Polish Jews, sometimes as Soviet. In some lists, some of them have probably not been counted at all, and in other lists, some of them may have been counted twice. One example of an area with a large Jewish population may illustrate these problems. Until 1939, the city of Vilna was part of Poland. Then it became part of Lithuania, which soon became part of the Soviet Union, and then, in June 1941, was invaded and occupied by Germany. In addition, Jews from other parts of Poland fled to Vilna between 1939 and 1941 to escape the Germans. It is not always clear whether these victims have been counted as Polish, Lithuanian, or Soviet Jews.

The same problems exist in other parts of Europe. Greek and Yugoslav Jews found they were now in Bulgaria. Austria became part of the German Reich as did parts of France and Poland. A section of Czechoslovakia (the Sudetenland) became part of Germany in 1938, while other areas were given to Hungary and Poland. The next year, the remaining Czech lands (Bohemia and Moravia) became a "protectorate" of Germany, and Slovakia became a separate country. Croatia became a separate country in 1941. About 150,000 Romanian Jews, and smaller numbers of Slovakian and Yugoslav Jews, lived in areas that became part of Hungary. Large numbers of Romanian Jews lived in a territory that was part of the Soviet Union between July 1940 and July 1941. Dawidowicz treats them as Romanians, and estimates the number of Romanian Jews killed as 300,000. But Bauer includes them with Soviet Jews, and his total for Romania is 40,000. Although some of these problems do not greatly affect an accurate estimate of the total number of victims, they do affect the accuracy of the number that is listed for each country.

The same is true of refugees. For example, there were over 500,000 Jews in Germany in 1933 when Adolf Hitler came to power. Several hundred thousand German Jews moved to other countries in Europe between 1933 and 1939. Most of these refugees were killed when the Nazis occupied their new countries. For example, around 30,000 were killed in the Netherlands alone. They are counted as Dutch Jews in most lists of victims, but this gives an unrealistic picture of the number of German Jewish victims. (In addition, thousands of German Jews were killed by the Nazis *before* the Holocaust. These are usually omitted from all lists.)

Keeping all these issues in mind, the following list of the number of people killed during the Holocaust cannot be perfectly accurate. However, it is based on the best recent estimates concerning each country. The numbers for Poland and the Soviet Union are the least certain. The numbers for the countries of western and northern Europe are the most exact. Except where otherwise noted, the totals refer to the September 1939 borders.

Country or Area	Number Killed
Austria 50,000	
(1937 borders; does not include refugees who resettled in other countries and were later killed.)	
Belgium 29,000	
Bulgaria . . . . ——	
(Includes only "Old Bulgaria"; approximately 14,000 Jews killed from areas that had been part of Greece [Thrace] and Yugoslavia [Macedonia].)	
Czech lands 78,000	
("Reich Protectorate of Bohemia and Moravia")	
Denmark 100	
Estonia 1,700	
France 77,000	
Germany 135,000	
(1937 borders plus Sudetenland; does not include Austria or refugees who resettled in other countries and were later killed.)	
Greece 64,000	
Hungary 550,000	
(Includes territory added from Czechoslovakia, Romania, and Yugoslavia beginning in 1938.)	
Italy 7,700	
Latvia 70,000	
Lithuania 140,000	
Luxembourg 2,000	
Netherlands 105,000	
Norway 750	
Poland 3,000,000	
(August 1939 borders, includes territory taken by Soviet Union in September 1939.)	
Romania 280,000	
(Does not include territory that became part of Hungary, but includes territory that Romania ceded to the Soviet Union from July 1940 until reoccupied by Romanian troops the following summer.)	
Slovakia 70,000	
Soviet Union 1,100,000	
(Does not include territory added from Poland in 1939 or Estonia, Latvia, and Lithuania.)	
Yugoslavia 60,000	
Total for Nazi-controlled Europe **5,820,250**	

HOLOCAUST Timeline

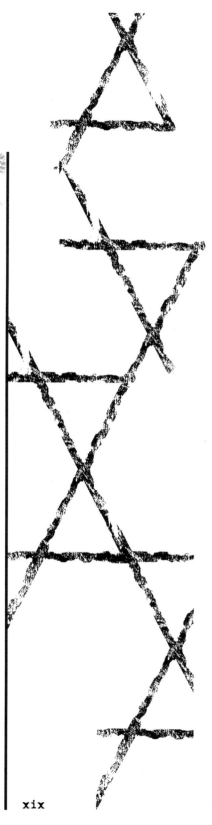

1871 Germany is unified under domination of the state of Prussia, and the German empire (Reich) is ruled by a kaiser (emperor).

1918 The German army is defeated by the Allies and revolution breaks out in Germany. The kaiser is overthrown and a republic is proclaimed on November 9. The new government agrees to an armistice, ending World War I, on November 11.

1919 Germany signs the Treaty of Versailles, which takes away territory, severely limits the size of the armed forces, and requires Germany to pay for war damage (reparations) and admit guilt for causing World War I. Extreme nationalist groups in Germany resent the treaty and blame socialists, communists, and Jews as a result.

1919 Adolf Hitler joins the tiny German Workers' Party in Munich. The party soon

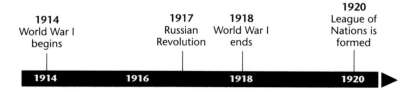

1914 World War I begins

1917 Russian Revolution

1918 World War I ends

1920 League of Nations is formed

1914 — 1916 — 1918 — 1920

changes its name to National Socialist German Workers' Party (NSDAP), called Nazi Party for short.

1922 Benito Mussolini and his Fascist Party march on Rome, then establish a dictatorship in Italy that becomes a model for Hitler.

1923 Adolf Hitler is in charge of the Beer Hall Putsch in Munich, the Nazis' attempt to take over the country. Police end the rebellion with gunfire, killing sixteen Nazis, injuring others, and arresting Hitler and other Nazi leaders.

1924 Hitler is sentenced to five years in prison for the Beer Hall Putsch, but serves only eight months, using the time to dictate *Mein Kampf* ("My Struggle"), which becomes the Nazi "bible."

1928 The Nazi Party receives about 800,000 votes in national elections, 2.6 percent of the total.

1930 The Nazis receive almost 6,500,000 votes in national elections and become the second-largest party in the Reichstag (German parliament.) As campaign tactics, storm troopers (SA or brownshirts), the military wing of the Nazi Party, attack opponents, break up meetings, and intimidate Jews.

1932 Although Hitler receives 11,000,000 votes in the first round of elections for German president, and over 13,000,000 million, almost 37 percent, in the second round, Paul von Hindenburg, the aged military hero of World War I, is reelected president. The Nazi storm troopers are briefly banned because of their increased violence during the campaign.

1933 Hitler becomes chancellor of Germany on January 30, but most of the government is made up of old-line conservatives who believe they can use and control the Nazis.

1925
The Scopes
"Monkey Trial"

1927
Charles Limbergh
completes first nonstop
solo transatlantic flight

1929
Great Depression
begins; it ends
in 1939

| 1925 | 1926 | 1927 | 1928 | 1929 |

1933 The Reichstag building is set on fire on February 27, and Hitler receives emergency powers from Hindenburg. Using police powers, storm troopers arrest 10,000 opponents of the Nazis, especially Communists, and send them to newly established concentration camps.

1933 The new Reichstag meets without Communist members who have been arrested or are in hiding. The Nazis and their allies win support from the Catholic parties and pass the "Enabling Act," giving Hitler dictatorial powers.

1933 The Nazis organize a national boycott of Jewish-owned businesses, and the first anti-Jewish laws are passed, removing almost all Jews from government jobs, including teaching. Further laws follow, and 53,000 Jews leave Germany during 1933.

1933 German labor unions are abolished and are replaced by the "German Labor Front," run by the Nazis. The Social Democratic Party (the largest party before the Nazi rise) is outlawed, then are all other parties. The Nazis conduct public book-burnings of works written by Jews and anti-Nazis.

1934 Hitler orders the murder of Ernst Röhm and other leaders of the SA (storm troopers), whom the German army fears as possible rivals, in what has become known as the "Night of Long Knives," June 30.

1934 Upon Hindenburg's death, Hitler combines the office of chancellor and president. Hitler is now the Führer (leader) of the Third Reich (Empire) with absolute powers.

1935 The German army enters the Rhineland, the area of western Germany that had been demilitarized by the Treaty of Versailles.

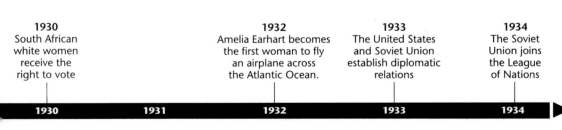

1930		1932	1933	1934
South African white women receive the right to vote		Amelia Earhart becomes the first woman to fly an airplane across the Atlantic Ocean.	The United States and Soviet Union establish diplomatic relations	The Soviet Union joins the League of Nations
1930	1931	1932	1933	1934

1935 The Nuremberg laws, followed by official decrees, define Jews in racial terms, strip them of German citizenship, and ban their marrying non-Jews.

1936 Buchenwald concentration camp is established.

1936 Hitler and the Nazis ease anti-Jewish actions as a result of the Olympic Games being held in Berlin, Germany's capital.

1936 Germany and Italy enter into agreements that develop into the "Rome-Berlin Axis," a political and military alliance of the two countries.

1938 German army moves into Austria, uniting the two countries in the *Anschluss*. Antisemitic laws are rapidly applied to Austria.

1938 An international conference is held in Evian, France, regarding the problems of Jewish refugees in Europe. Nothing is done to resolve the crisis.

1938 At a Munich conference, leaders of France and Britain agree to give Germany a section of Czechoslovakia that contains a large German minority.

1938 In Paris, Hershel Grynszpan, a young Jew, shoots and kills Ernst vom Rath, an official at the German embassy. Grynszpan's actions spark *Kristallnacht* ("Crystal Night"), the organized Nazi attacks throughout Germany in which Jews are beaten, synagogues are burned, Jewish businesses are destroyed, and 30,000 Jewish men are arrested and sent to concentration camps.

1939 Hitler violates the Munich agreement by destroying the remainder of Czechoslovakia and implements anti-Jewish measures.

1939 Nazi Germany and the Soviet Union sign the Nazi-Soviet Pact, in which the two countries promise not to attack each other and secretly agree to divide Poland.

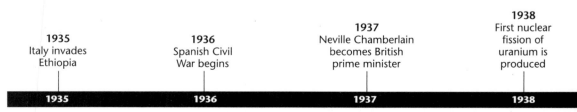

1935
Italy invades
Ethiopia

1936
Spanish Civil
War begins

1937
Neville Chamberlain
becomes British
prime minister

1938
First nuclear
fission of
uranium is
produced

1935 1936 1937 1938

1939 World War II begins when Germany invades Poland on September 1, and Britain and France retaliate by declaring war on Germany two days later.

1939 Beginning of the Nazi "euthanasia" ("mercy killing") program, in which 70,000 mentally and physically handicapped Germans, including children, are murdered.

1939 Reinhard Heydrich, second in command of the SS, the Nazi Party' military wing, issues an order for the concentration of all Polish Jews into large ghettos as the first step towards the unnamed "final aim."

1939 Jews in German-occupied Poland are ordered to wear a yellow star (the Star of David) at all times.

1940 Heinrich Himmler, head of the SS, orders the building of a concentration camp at Auschwitz in occupied Poland.

1940 French troops evacuate Paris on June 13, and German forces enter the city the next day. France signs an armistice with Germany, and German troops occupy northern France, while a government friendly to Germany (Vichy France) has some independence in the south. Anti-Jewish measures soon begin in western European countries controlled by Germany.

1940 The Warsaw ghetto in Poland is sealed and about 450,000 Jews are confined within its walls.

1941 Germany invades the Soviet Union during "Operation Barbarossa." Special murder squads, called *Einsatzgruppen*, follow the Germany army into the Soviet Union.

1941 Hermann Göring, second to Hitler in Nazi hierarchy, gives Reinhard Heydrich the authority "to carry out all necessary preparations . . . for a total solution of the Jewish question" throughout Nazi-controlled Europe.

1941 Six hundred Soviet prisoners of war and 250 Poles are the victims of the first gassings at Auschwitz.

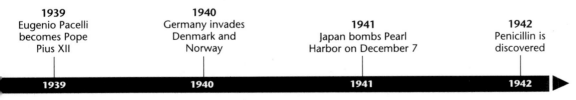

1939
Eugenio Pacelli becomes Pope Pius XII

1940
Germany invades Denmark and Norway

1941
Japan bombs Pearl Harbor on December 7

1942
Penicillin is discovered

1939 — 1940 — 1941 — 1942

1941 On September 29 and 30, 33,000 Jews are machine-gunned at Babi Yar outside the city of Kiev, Ukraine.

1941 Construction begins on Birkenau (Auschwitz II) in Poland, the largest Nazi death camp.

1941 The death camp at Chelmno, in the western part of Poland that had been annexed to Germany, begins operation. Jews are gassed in sealed vans.

1942 Reinhard Heydrich calls the Wannsee Conference, where the "Final Solution" is transmitted to various branches of German government.

1942 Slovakian Jews become the first from outside of Poland to be transported to Auschwitz.

1942 Reinhard Heydrich is fatally wounded in an attack by Czech resistance fighters.

1942 The Treblinka death camp begins receiving the Jews of Warsaw. It is the last of the three camps, along with Belzec and Sobibór, that are created to exterminate the Jews of Poland. The Nazis call this "Operation Reinhard," in honor of the assassinated Heydrich.

1943 German attempts to deport Danish Jews are defeated when almost the entire Jewish population of Denmark is safely transported to Sweden.

1943 The Germans occupy Hungary and begin large-scale deportations of Hungarian Jews. By July, 400,000 Hungarian Jews have been sent to Auschwitz.

1943 A small group of German army officers wishing to end the war unsuccessfully try to assassinate Hitler. Many of them, along with their families, are tortured and executed as a result.

1943 The Soviet army enters Lublin in eastern Poland and liberates the nearby Majdanek death camp. The Soviets

1943 Allies occupy Naples, Italy		1947 State of Israel is declared	1949 Israel is admitted to the United Nations	1954 Vietnam War begins
	1945 V-E Day			
1943	**1945**	**1947**	**1949**	**1951**

capture much of the camp, and many documents, before they can be destroyed.

1943 The Polish underground launches a full-scale uprising against the Germans in the Warsaw ghetto. Savage fighting continues in the city for two months until the resistance is finally crushed.

1945 As Soviet troops approach, the Nazis begin the evacuation of Auschwitz. Almost 60,000 surviving prisoners are forced on a death march.

1945 American troops liberate the Buchenwald and Dachau concentration camps, and British troops free the Bergen-Belsen concentration camp.

1945 Hitler commits suicide in his fortified bunker beneath Berlin, and Germany surrenders.

1946 Hermann Göring, one of the highest Nazi officials to be accused and convicted of war crimes, testifies on his behalf during the Nuremberg Trials.

1962 Former Nazi official Adolf Eichmann is executed after being found guilty of war crimes for his part in the murder of hundreds of thousands of Jews.

1985 Human remains found in Brazil are confirmed to be those of Nazi doctor Josef Mengele, who performed inhumane experiments on the prisoners of Auschwitz.

1987 Former SS soldier Klaus Barbie is found guilty of crimes against humanity and is sentenced to life in prison.

1998 The Vatican issues a letter stating that Pope Pius XII, leader of the Catholic Church during the Holocaust, did all he could to save the Jews.

1998 Maurice Papon, a former official of the Vichy government, is sentenced to ten years in prison for helping the Germans illegally arrest and deport French Jews.

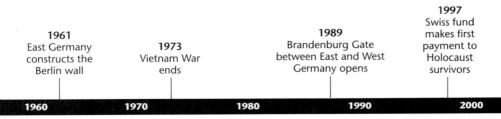

1961
East Germany constructs the Berlin wall

1973
Vietnam War ends

1989
Brandenburg Gate between East and West Germany opens

1997
Swiss fund makes first payment to Holocaust survivors

| 1960 | 1970 | 1980 | 1990 | 2000 |

Words to Know

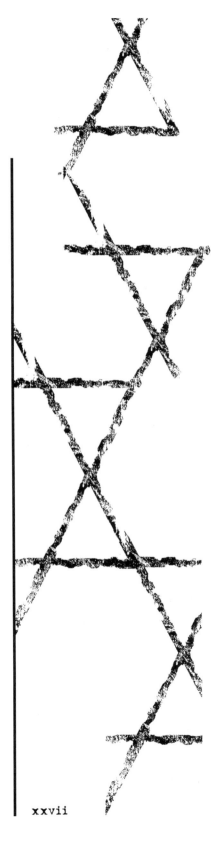

A

Aktion: The German term for the roundup and murder of Jews.

Allies: The countries of Great Britain, the United States, the Soviet Union, and France, who fought against Germany, Italy, and Japan during World War II.

Antisemetism: The hatred of Jews, who are sometimes called Semites.

Anschluss: The German invasion and annexation of Austria in 1938.

Aryans: A term originally used for the peoples speaking the languages of Europe and India. The Nazis used the term to mean anyone who was non-Jewish and of Germanic background.

Aryanization: The Nazi process of seizing the property of Jews and selling it to non-Jews.

B

Bliztkrieg: The military strategy of troops in land vehicles making quick, surprise strikes against the enemy with support from airplanes.

Bund: A Polish Jewish resistance group.

C

Chancellor: The head of the German government.

Collaborators: People who turned their own friends, families, and neighbors over to the Nazis.

Communism: An economic system that promotes the ownership of all property by the community as a whole.

Concentration camps: Places where the Nazis confined people they regarded as "enemies of the state."

Crematoriums: Buildings that held large ovens used to dispose of the bodies of dead concentration camp inmates.

Crimes against humanity: Murder, extermination, enslavement, deportation, and other acts committed against the nonmilitary population of a country.

D

D-Day: The name given to June 6, 1944, the day that British and American forces landed on the beaches of Normandy in northern France.

Death march: The process of forcing long rows of prisoners to walk great distances without the proper food or clothing.

Democracy: A system of government in which the people elect their rulers.

Deportation: The process by which Nazis forcibly removed people from their normal place of residence to a labor, concentration, or death camp.

Depression: An economic downturn.

Dictator: A person holding absolute ruling power in a country.

E

Einsatzgruppen: Special mobile units of the SS and SD that followed the German army into the Soviet Union; they shot at least 1,000,000 Jews.

Emigration: The act of leaving one's country to settle in another.

Euthanasia: The act of killing people whom the Nazis considered "unfit to live."

F

Fascism: A system of government that is marked by dictatorship, government control of the economy, and suppression of all opposition.

Final Solution: The code name given to the Nazi plan to totally eliminate the Jews of Europe.

Free Corps: Or *Freikorps;* volunteer units made up mostly of former officers and professional soldiers. Munch of the SA was made up of former Free Corps members.

Führer: The German word meaning "leader."

G

Gassing: The Nazi process of locking people in sealed rooms and then filling the rooms with poisonous gas in order to suffocate the people to death.

Genocide: The deliberate, systematic destruction of a racial, cultural, or political group.

Gentiles: Non-Jewish people.

Gestapo: An abbreviation for *Geheime Staats Politzei* or German secret police.

Ghettos: Crowded, walled sections of cities where Jews were forced to live in inferior conditions.

Gypsies: Dark-haired, dark-skinned, nomadic people who are believed to have originated in India. They are sometimes also called Roma or Sinti.

H

Holocaust: The period between 1933 and 1945 when Nazi Germany systematically persecuted and murdered millions of Jews, Gypsies, homosexuals, Jehovah's Witnesses, and other innocent people.

Home Army: A Polish secret military resistance organization.

I

Inflation: A continuing rise in prices, caused by an abnormal increase in the amount of money or credit available.

J

Jehovah's Witnesses: A religious group whose beliefs did not allow them to swear allegiance to any worldly power.

Judenrat: The German term for Jewish Council. Nazi leaders ordered the formation of Jewish Councils in the ghettos.

Junkers: Powerful German nobles.

K

Kaiser: The German word for "emperor."

Kapos: Prisoners who worked for the Nazis.

L

Lebensraum: The Nazi idea that the German people or Aryan race needed expanded living space to survive.

Liquidation: The Nazi process of destroying a ghetto by first sending prisoners to death camps and then burning the buildings.

Luftwaffe: The German air force.

N

Nationalists: People who have an intense feeling of loyalty and devotion to a nation.

Nazi: The abbreviation for the National Socialist German Worker's Party.

Neo-Nazis: People who idolize the Nazis and their policies today.

O

Occupation: Control of a country by a foreign military power.

Operation Reinhard: The name given to the Nazi plan to physically eliminate all the Jews of Europe. The name was in honor of Reinhard Heydrich, the architect of the Final Solution.

P

Partisans: Fighters who attack the enemy within occupied territory.

Passive resistance: Resistance to a government by nonviolent methods.

Pogroms: Mass attacks against a particular group of people.

Propaganda: Official government communications to the public that are designed to influence opinion. The information may be true or false.

Prussia: The largest state of the German empire from 1871 to 1918.

Putsch: An unsuccessful attempt to overthrow a government.

R

Rabbi: A Jewish religious leader.

Reds: Slang term for people who practice Communism.

Refugees: People who flee to a foreign country to escape danger and persecution.

Reich: The German word for "empire."

Reichstag: Germany's parliament or lawmaking body.

Resistance: Working against an occupying army.

Reparations: Compensation paid by a defeated nation for damage they caused to another country during a war.

Resettlement: The Nazi term for forcing Jews into ghettos and concentration camps.

S

SA: An abbreviation for *Sturmabteilungen,* or storm troopers. They were members of a special armed and uniformed branch of the Nazi Party.

Sabotage: The deliberate destruction of an enemy's property or equipment during wartime.

SD: An abbreviation for *Sicherdienst,* or Security Police. This unit served as the intelligence (spy) service of the SS.

Selection: The process by which the Nazis decided who would be spared to work and who would be killed immediately.

Socialism: A political and economic system based on government control of the production and distribution of goods.

Sonderkommando: Jewish prisoners who were forced to dispose of bodies of gassed inmates by cremation.

Soviet Union: Present day Russia; a former Communist country of eastern Europe and northern Asia that was founded in 1917 after the Russian government was overthrown. The Soviet Union, formally known as the Union of Socialist Republics, was dissolved in 1991.

SS: An abbreviation for *Shutzstaffeln,* or Security Squad. This unit provided Hitler's personal bodyguards and guards for the various concentration camps.

Storm troopers: Another name given to members of the SA.

Swastika: The Nazi symbol of a black, bent-armed cross that always appeared within a white circle and set on a red background.

Synagogue: A Jewish place of worship.

T

Third Reich: The name Hitler gave to his term as Germany's leader. It means "Third Empire."

Treaty of Versailles: The restrictive treaty that Germany was forced to sign by the Allies after World War I.

Typhus: A serious disease, usually transmitted by body lice, that is marked by a high fever, intense headache, and dark red rash.

U

Underground: Engaged in secret or illegal activity.

W

Waffen-SS: The military unit of the Nazi political police.

Wannsee Conference: The conference called by Reinhard

Heydrich in 1941 to inform branches of the German government about the "Final Solution."

War crimes: Violations of the laws or customs of war.

Weimar Republic: Democratic government imposed upon Germany at the end of World War I.

Y

Yiddish: A language spoken by Eastern European Jews.

Yom Kippur: A Jewish holy day that is accompanied by fasting and praying for the atonement of sins.

Z

Zionists: People who supported the creation of a Jewish nation in Palestine.

ZOB: The initials for *Zydowsk Organizacja Bojowa,* the military wing of the Jewish underground in the Warsaw ghetto.

Zyklon B: A highly poisonous insecticide that the Nazis used in the gas chambers to kill the victims locked inside.

Understanding
the
HOLOCAUST

8

The Death Camps

T he organized murder of the Jewish people of Europe began in the spring of 1941. Hundreds of thousands of Jews had died in mass shootings carried out by the *Einsatzgruppen,* "special groups" that followed the German army as it invaded Russia. (See Chapter 7, pp.186–88.) But this was not enough. There were about 11 million Jews in Europe. The great majority of them were concentrated in areas controlled by Nazi Germany. Even the mass shootings by the *Einsatzgruppen,* could not kill this enormous number of people quickly or efficiently enough to meet the Nazi Party's goals.

Mass shootings posed additional problems for the Nazis. For one thing, they required too much manpower. And it would take even more Nazi shooters to increase the scale of killings to the level the Nazis wanted to attain. Murder by shooting could not be kept secret enough, either. Too many people had to participate, and too many outsiders could hear the shots and see

Prisoners from Buchenwald concentration camp await execution in a forest. The Nazis soon determined that mass shooting was not an efficient way to kill Jews.

the bodies of the dead. Killing people in this way was also too personal. The shooters saw each individual they killed, including women and children. The men assigned to pull the trigger eventually suffered from serious psychological problems. Even though they had been trained to kill (and to believe that Jews were not human), the stress and horror of their assignment caused some of them to experience mental breakdowns.

If the mass shootings became widely known, Jews who anticipated their fate might resist or try to escape; they had nothing to lose. So the Nazis decided that the killing of the Jews should not be done openly. Instead, the Jews would be taken away for "resettlement" to some vague place "in the east" and killed there. The killing would be kept secret, it would take fewer people to accomplish, and it would be finished faster.

By concealing the mass murders, the Nazis would not have to worry about members of the non-Jewish population

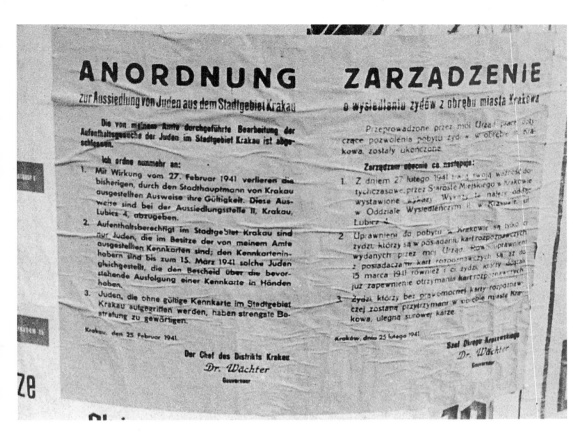

A close-up of an announcement ordering the "resettlement" of Jews from the Polish city of Kraków in 1941.

coming to the aid of the Jews. Many people in eastern Europe were prejudiced against the Jewish people and probably wouldn't have objected to the Jews being forced from their homes and sent away to an unknown location. But even the most bigoted German might protest the Nazi Party's practice of shooting Jewish men, women—even babies—in cold blood. It was one thing to know that the Jews were being persecuted and segregated, but very different to know through real experience that they were being brutally murdered as part of a government policy. Taking the Jews away to be killed allowed people who really didn't want to know what was happening to the Jews to make sure that they didn't find out. Denial and blind obedience on the part of the German populace probably assisted the Nazis more than anything else.

"Operation Reinhard"

The Nazis decided that the first region to be "cleansed" of Jews would be the General Government, the name they gave to what was left of Poland after most of western Poland became part of Germany. The General Government was run completely by German officials; there were no Poles in any of the region's government positions. Poland had been the home of the largest number of Jews in Europe. According to the Germans, the General Government alone still contained 2,284,000 Jews. In addition, Jews from all over the rest of Europe were being moved into the General Government every day.

The plan to kill the Jews of the General Government was called "Operation Reinhard" ("Aktion Reinhard" in German). It was named for Reinhard Heydrich, the man who had coordinated the Wannsee Conference, where the so-called "Final Solution"—the mass murder of the Jews of Europe—had been officially decided. (See pp. 204-08.) Heydrich was second in command of the *Schutzstaffel,* or SS, the military organization of the Nazi Party that was in charge of anti-Jewish actions. He had been chosen to carry out the Final Solution. In May 1942, Heydrich was assassinated by resistance fighters in Czechoslovakia. The Nazis "honored" him by giving his name to the largest murder plan ever devised.

The murder plan begins with the ghettos

As in other parts of Poland, the Jews of the territory of the General Government were concentrated into ghettos, special areas in the cities and towns where people of Jewish heritage were forced to live. (See Chapters 5 and 6 for more information about Jewish ghettos in Poland.)

After all the Jews were gathered in ghettos, they were eventually sent by train for "resettlement." Usually, they were told they were being sent to "the east"—to territory the German army had captured from Russia. In the smaller ghettos, this shuffling process might take only a day or two. All of the Jews were forced onto trains until the ghetto was empty. The Nazis called this "liquidating" the ghetto. In larger ghettos, the process took months. A few thousand people would be sent away at a time until all of them were gone. But these Jews were not being "resettled." They were being sent to their deaths.

The death camps

The trains took the Jews of Poland to special camps. These camps were different from the older concentration

camps in Germany. The concentration camps were places where the Nazis sent prisoners, including Jews, sometimes for years. The prisoners were horribly mistreated, underfed, and forced to work under subhuman conditions for endless hours. Sanitation was terrible, and medical care was almost nonexistent. Many prisoners died of diseases that swept through the camps or simply from exhaustion and malnutrition. Many others were brutally beaten for breaking some minor rule—or just on an SS officer's whim. Some were shot or hanged, either as a punishment or, again, because a Nazi felt like killing a Jew.

As terrible as the concentration camps were, the new death camps in Poland were worse. In these places death was not something that *might* happen; it was planned, organized, and carried out with efficiency. Eventually, there were six places set up for mass murder by the Nazis. Hundreds of thousands of Jews were killed in each one.

Jews of the Lódz ghetto on their way to the train station, where they will be herded into cars and sent to the Auschwitz death camp.

Prisoners working on a rifle production line in the SS-owned munitions factory at Dachau, the first concentration camp.

In two of them, Majdanek and Auschwitz, there were also many non-Jewish victims, especially Poles and captured Russian soldiers. These two camps, where 1.5 million people died, also had huge slave-labor systems. Tens of thousands of prisoners worked in factories at the camps, making items needed for the German war effort. Like the prisoners in the older concentration camps, these inmates were constantly beaten, nearly starved, and died by the thousands of disease. The prisoners in Majdanek and Auschwitz were killed as soon as they became too weak to work. (See Chapter 9 for more information on Auschwitz.)

The other four camps—Chelmno, Belzec, Sobibór, and Treblinka—were built for the single purpose of killing Jews. They were not meant to serve any other function. The prisoners were not put to work—except to help run the killing process. And, unlike Auschwitz, these camps did not have vast number of prisoners because each trainload of Jews was killed as soon as possible. These four places killed over 2 million Jews.

Chelmno

Chelmno (Kulmhof in German) began to operate in December 1941 about 35 miles from the city of Lódz. It was not in the General Government but in the part of Poland that had been made part of Germany.

The Nazis used a method of killing at Chelmno they had devised during the Russian invasion. People were sent by train to designated railroad stations and then taken to Chelmno on trucks. There they were forced into the back of a truck that looked like a furniture van. The Nazis crammed as many persons into each truck as could possibly fit. The back was sealed so that no air could enter. Next, the exhaust from the truck engine was directed into the back through a hose. The engine of the truck was turned on, sending carbon monoxide into the truck. This continued until all the people inside were dead from carbon monoxide poisoning. Then the truck was driven to the nearby forest, and the bodies were dumped into mass graves.

The Nazis repeated this procedure over and over. An estimated 340,000 people died at Chelmno, including about 5,000 Roma (Gypsies) and hundreds of Poles. It was also at Chelmno that the Nazis murdered many of the children of the village of Lidice, Czechoslovakia. The Nazis had destroyed Lidice to avenge the assassination of Reinhard Heydrich.

The rest of the victims at Chelmno, a third of a million people, were Jews. Only three people who were sent there are known to have survived.

Designing a killing factory

Chelmno was considered an advancement in the killing process. It surpassed mass shootings in ease and efficiency. But it still was not good enough for the Nazis. Although each truck was loaded as tightly as possible, the killing could not keep up with the great numbers of intended victims.

So the people in charge of Operation Reinhard built three new camps, each one located near a large center of Jew-

What the Numbers Mean

A large baseball stadium holds about 55,000 people. If everyone in that stadium were murdered, and if the stadium were filled up again five more times, and all of those people were also murdered, that would still be less than the number of Jews killed at Chelmno alone.

An average American classroom holds about 30 students. If all the students in 8,000 classrooms were killed, that would still be less than the number of Jews killed at Sobibór.

If every person who lives in the city of Denver, Colorado, were killed, and then every person who lives in Pittsburgh, Pennsylvania, that total would still be less than the number of Jews killed at Treblinka.

If all the people living in the cities of Philadelphia, Pennsylvania; San Diego, California; Detroit, Michigan; Dallas, Texas; and Baltimore, Maryland, were killed, that would still be less than the number of Jews killed by the Nazis.

ish population. But they were far enough away, and hidden well enough in the forests, so that the activities within could be kept secret. The camps were strategically located on railroad lines. Trains arrived first from Poland and then from all over Europe—Holland, Greece, and France, as well as Russia and Germany.

The camps were staffed by relatively few people—about 20 or 30 SS men. Almost all of them were veterans of the Nazis' euthanasia program, the killing of thousands of mentally retarded and disabled Germans, including children. (See pp. 108–14.) They were well experienced in killing innocent people for the purpose of keeping Germany "pure." In addition, each camp had between 90 and 120 armed Ukrainian guards. These men were soldiers in the Soviet (Russian) army who had been captured by the Germans and had volunteered to help the Nazis.

Learning from Chelmno: Three more places of death

Three new camps were designed for killing people as quickly as possible.

The first camp was called Belzec. It was located between the cities of Lublin and Lwów (Lvov) and operated from February to December 1942. About 600,000 people died at Belzec. Almost all were Jewish. Only two people survived.

Sobibór was situated east of Lublin. It operated from May 1942 through October 1943. An estimated 250,000 people died at Sobibór. Almost all were Jewish. Sixty-four people survived.

Treblinka was located near Warsaw—the capital of Poland and the city with the most Jews. It was the last of the three camps to begin its work. The Nazis used what they had learned at the other camps to "improve" on processes at Tre-

Ukrainian guards march at a concentration camp. The Ukrainian guards were Soviet soldiers who volunteered to help their captors, the Germans, at the camps.

blinka—to make it the most efficient killing center of all. Treblinka operated from July 1942 to August 1943. In the first five weeks it was open, over 312,000 people were killed there. All together, about 870,000 people were murdered at Treblinka. Almost all were Jewish. Somewhere between 40 and 70 people survived.

Assembly lines of murder

In less than two years, 1.75 million people were killed in these three camps together. A horrible efficiency prevailed; less than 450 men worked in the death camps. In Treblinka alone, 70,000 people a month were murdered with less than 30 SS men in charge.

The Nazis considered the killing of Jews a technical problem and approached its solution in the same way an automobile manufacturer might figure out a way for more cars to be assembled on each line every hour. Each aspect of the killings was thought out. The Nazi murderers carefully planned the best way to transport the Jews to the camps, how to deal with them when they arrived at those camps, and then exactly how to kill them. They planned out all the details, such as how to get rid of their clothes, their possessions, and finally, their bodies.

The transports

The small number of Nazis and Ukrainian guards at Belzec, Sobibór, and Treblinka were able to control thousands of victims at a time. One reason for this was that the Jews who arrived at the camps had already suffered almost unbelievable conditions on the transport trains that brought them to the camps. They arrived exhausted, starving, desperate for water. Many had died on the trip. When the survivors were finally allowed off the trains, they were told they had reached a transit camp, a stop along the way to resettlement. Even among those who suspected that the "resettlement" was a lie, many must have wanted to believe that they were mistaken.

Among the descriptions of these transports were several written by officers of the German reserve police who guarded many of the trains. In *Ordinary Men: Reserve Police Battalion 101 and the Final Solution*, historian Christopher R. Browning collects some of these reports, describing the terrible journeys

forced upon the Jews of Nazi-occupied Europe from the Nazi point of view.

A transport to Belzec

Browning's work includes a German police officer's descriptions of two separate transports, a few days apart in 1942, from the town of Kolomyja, in Galicia, the southeastern part of Poland. There had been mass shootings of Jews in Galicia the year before. Because of this, the Jews of the area most likely concluded that they, too, were going to be killed. Although the Jews were told they were being transported as a

A German soldier oversees Jews being deported in 1942. The Nazis carefully planned the transporting of Jews to the camps, how to deal with them upon arrival, and how to kill them.

Nazi Priorities: Killing Before Winning

For the Nazi government, destroying the Jewish people was even more important than winning World War II. The use of German trains to transport Jews is a clear example of this. Records indicate that there was sometimes a serious shortage of trains to take German soldiers and equipment to fight in the Soviet Union. At the same time, hundreds of locomotives and cars were being used to transport Jews to be slaughtered in the death camps. The army actually tried to suspend the death trains temporarily, but they were stopped by Heinrich Himmler, the head of the SS (the Nazi's military arm charged with eliminating the Jews), who was considered the second most powerful man in Germany. Hitler himself must have agreed.

Many Jews were forced to work for the German army in war industries. In Latvia and Lithuania, for example, most skilled construction workers were Jews. The German administrators of the area knew these workers could not be replaced by non-Jews. But the Nazi government made it clear that the killing of the Jews must go ahead, even if it hurt the army. "Economic considerations," the government ordered, "should be overlooked in the solution of the problem."

By the fall of 1942, there were more than 1,000,000 laborers in Poland working in German war industries. Over 300,000 of them were Jews—and a third of that number, or 100,000, were skilled workers. The military commander in the General Government argued that it was impossible to replace these workers, and that removing them would "considerably reduce" the German army's ability to win the war. Himmler sent a memo to top SS leaders, with copies to army officers. The Jews employed in war industries would be sent to concentration camps, regardless of its effect on the war. The army did as it was told.

part of the overall plan requiring the "resettlement" of Jews, the Nazis suspected that these Jews might take great risks to escape.

The Jews of Kolomyja had been ordered to report for "registration" at 5:30 on the morning of September 7, 1942. About 5,300 did so. As Lieutenant Westermann of the reserve police wrote in his report, his company then surrounded the ghetto "and searched thoroughly, whereby some 600 additional Jews were hunted down."

It took until 7:00 that evening to complete the loading of the train. "Each car of the transport was loaded with 100 Jews. The great heat prevailing that day made the entire operation very difficult," Lieutenant Westermann reported. The cars were sealed and their doors nailed shut, as usual, he

Loaded transport trains arrive at one of the death camps in May 1944. Conditions in the boxcars were unbearable.

explained. But because it was already dark by the time the train left at 9:00, and because of the great heat, "many Jews escaped by squeezing through the air holes after removing the barbed wire [that covered them]. While the guard was able to shoot many of them immediately, most of the escaping Jews were eliminated that night or the next day by the railroad guard or other police units." Although the train reached Belzec without any further incident, Lieutenant Westermann complained in his report that the guard of one officer and nine men was not enough.

The day after the transport left Kolomyja, Lieutenant Westermann wrote, "some 300 Jews—old and weak, ill, frail, and no longer transportable—were executed." Demonstrating the incredible detail with which the Nazis planned for the efficient and cost-effective extermination of the Jews, the lieutenant carefully explained that he had obeyed a recent order concerning the use of ammunition: "90% of those executed were shot with carbines and rifles. Only in exceptional cases were pistols used."

The second transport from Kolomyja to Belzec

As soon as most of the Jews of Kolomyja had been sent to their deaths, the Jews from the surrounding area were brought to the vacated town. Some of them were marched more than 30 miles on foot. While waiting overnight in the town, many were shot by German guards. The surviving Jews were loaded into 30 freight cars. Lieutenant Westermann described the conditions in his report: "Given the great heat prevailing on those days and the strain on the Jews from the long foot marches or from waiting for days without being given any provisions worth noting, the excessively great overloading of the cars with 180 to 200 Jews was catastrophic in a way that had tremendously adverse effects on the transport." Lieutenant Westermann was not worried about what was happening to the people inside the cars, but about running a smooth operation.

The 30 cars loaded in Kolomyja were attached to 20 other cars that had already been loaded in two nearby towns. The train contained 8,205 people. The heat was stifling and everyone in the cars removed their clothing. Night fell as the train waited for the cars to be nailed shut and the small air holes to be covered with barbed wire "in the usual regulation manner."

The Jews tried again and again to escape from the train. "Breakout attempts from the parked train could not be prevented in the darkness, nor could the escaping Jews be shot in flight," reported Lieutenant Westermann.

When the train finally moved out of the town, the prisoners continued to attempt to escape by breaking through the sides and the roofs of some of the cars. The train stopped at several stations along the way so that the holes through which the Jews were escaping could be boarded up.

There were only ten German guards, five at each end of the train. They shot as many of the escapees as they could. Before the train reached Belzec, the guards used up all their ammunition, as well as extra ammunition they had gotten from soldiers along the way. They used bayonets on the escaping Jews when the train was stopped but could only

throw rocks at those who were able to jump off the train while it was moving.

"Because of the special circumstances described," Lieutenant Westermann wrote, "the number of Jews who escaped from this transport cannot be specified. Nonetheless, it can be assumed that at least two-thirds of the escaping Jews were shot or rendered harmless in some other way."

When the train reached Belzec, 2,000 of the Jews were already dead from suffocation or heat prostration from the overly hot environment.

Arrival

When the transport trains reached the death camps, the first 20 freight cars were brought to the unloading area while the others waited farther away. Belzec, Sobibór, and Treblinka were disguised as transit camps, so the victims who arrived at

Jewish police assist Jews boarding a deportation train.

Deception

At Treblinka, where the Jews of Warsaw were sent, there was a large printed sign that read:

Jews of Warsaw, Attention!

You are in a transit camp, from which you will be sent to a labor camp. In order to avoid epidemics, you must present your clothing and belongings for immediate disinfection. Gold, money, foreign currency, and jewelry should be deposited with the cashiers in return for a receipt. They will be returned to you later when you present the receipt. Bodily cleanliness requires that everyone bathe before continuing the journey.

The first building that the Jews saw was disguised as a typical small-town railroad station. It had signs that pointed to the waiting room, to the ticket office, and to the trains for various destinations. But there was no waiting room or ticket office, and there were no other tracks. A clock hung on the wall, but it was not a real clock; the hands were merely painted on.

these places did not realize this was their final destination. They were told these were only stops along their route and that they would continue their voyage to "resettlement," or to a labor camp, after they were processed. One SS man said after the war that the Jews who arrived at Sobibór had no idea what was happening to them until they were actually inside the gas chamber.

The camps were not very large. Treblinka and Sobibór were rectangles of about 400 by 600 yards. It would only have taken about 20 or 25 minutes to walk all the way around the camp. Belzec was even smaller, a square less than 300 yards long on each side. The camps were surrounded by barbed-wire fences, with high watchtowers at the corners. Tree branches and leaves in the fencing prevented anyone from seeing through.

When the first 20 cars stopped at the unloading area, the doors were opened by a group of prisoners. All the Jews were ordered out. The prisoners who opened the doors were men, usually young and healthy, who had arrived on an earlier transport and had not been killed.

The SS men and the Ukrainian guards marched the new arrivals into the camp as quickly as possible. Anyone who lagged behind was beaten with a rifle butt or whipped.

Meanwhile, the prisoners who had opened the cars removed the bodies of those who had died on the train. Then they cleaned the cars. Blood, vomit, and human waste were washed away. Bits of clothing or personal possessions left behind were swept out. In a few minutes, all evidence of what had happened on the train was erased.

Processing

When the people who had just gotten off the train entered the camp, they were told to leave all their belongings behind. Any suitcases they had kept were taken from them. All valuables, such as money or jewels, that they had brought to help them "resettle" were collected. Then the men were separated from the women and children.

The women and children were marched to a long barrack or building. There they were ordered to undress completely so that they could be disinfected in the shower houses. They were also told to tie their shoes together with the piece of string provided them.

After this, the women had their hair cut off by prisoners. Again, the excuse given was to prevent disease. In fact the hair was used to make products for the German armed forces, such as water-resistant rope for the navy.

When the haircutting was done, the guards beat and whipped the women and children, still naked, to force them to run through a narrow path between barbed-wire fences. Like the fence outside the camp, these were camouflaged with tree branches to prevent anyone from seeing through. The path was about a hundred yards long. It was called "the tube."

The Nazis also called the path "the road to heaven." It was their idea of a joke. There was a sign along the path that read: "To the showers." The path led to the part of the camp that was hidden from the arriving passengers. This part of the camp was the place where the killing was done.

Concentration camp inmates walk near a large pile of shoes of those prisoners who were "processed."

While the women were being "processed," the men waited. They too were naked. After a while, perhaps half an hour or more, they were forced to run to the tube and through it.

On the other side of the path was a building. Inside the building were the gas chambers.

The gas chambers

In each of the camps, the building that held the gas chambers was made to look like a public bathhouse, which was a familiar sight in Europe in that period. As they came through the tube, the prisoners were forced to enter the building through the main door. Inside were doors to smaller rooms, where shower heads hung from the ceiling. These rooms also had doors leading to the outside of the building, but they were sealed.

"The Infirmary"

Many of the Jews were too weak from hunger and disease to walk to the gas chambers, even under the threat of beatings. In Treblinka, these people were carried on stretchers by the prisoners to a small building. The building had a sign that said it was a field hospital or infirmary and was marked with a red cross.

On the other side of the building, there was a wall of earth 15 feet high. Behind this wall, hidden from view from the sorting area or the barracks where people undressed, was a large open pit. The back of the infirmary building was near the edge of this pit. One by one, the sick were taken out of the "infirmary" through the back and immediately shot by one of the Ukrainian guards. Then the guard pushed each dead body into the pit.

In Treblinka, there were originally three of these rooms, each a square only about 13 feet on each side. The Jews were packed into these three rooms as tightly as possible. Two hundred people were forced into each one, and then the rooms were sealed.

Next, the engine of a captured Russian tank was turned on. The carbon monoxide gas from the engine was pumped through the shower heads into the sealed rooms. For half an hour the gas poured in. The people inside gasped and coughed and choked. They clawed desperately to escape. Their bodies were drenched with sweat, with blood, with their own waste. They did not even have room to fall down when they died. They died pressed against each other, their bodies tangled together.

This is how the gas chambers worked at Treblinka. Later, in October 1942, ten new gas chambers were added there. Instead of being able to hold about 600 people, the gas chambers could now kill 3,800 people at one time. In one day, up to 15,000 people could be murdered.

The rear side of a gas chamber. The engine to the right was used to create carbon monoxide for gassing prisoners.

Disposal

After everyone inside had died, the outside doors to the gas chambers were opened by a special group of the "permanent" prisoners. They had to separate the bodies and remove them. Other prisoners washed out the gas chambers to ready them for the next victims.

Meanwhile, other prisoners, known as the "dentists," searched the mouths of the dead for gold teeth and fillings and removed them with pliers. Then the bodies were carried to several giant pits located about 150 to 200 yards from the gas chambers. They were thrown into the pits and buried. The next group of victims would be thrown on top of them.

In March 1943, Heinrich Himmler, the head of the SS, visited Treblinka. He did not like the fact that hundreds of thousands of bodies were buried there and in the other death camps of Operation Reinhard. The bodies were evidence of what the Nazis had done. The German armies were beginning to lose the war against the Soviet Union. Although the Soviet army was still far away, it was possible that Russian soldiers would reach the death camps of Poland someday. Therefore, Himmler ordered the burning of all the bodies buried at the camps.

Prisoners dug up the buried bodies and placed them on steel rails that had been laid on top of concrete pillars. The Nazis brought a large crane to Treblinka to dig up the bodies faster. Prisoners arranged the dead on the rails. Corpses were piled on top of each other in layers, with dry wood underneath. Two thousand bodies could be placed on the pile at one time.

The work went on all day. Then the pile of corpses was set on fire. The fire burned all night. The next morning, the ashes were mixed with sand and buried in deep ditches. Those body parts that had not been burned completely had to be placed on the pile again.

Eventually, there were six of these giant grills at Treblinka. About 12,000 bodies could be burned at one time. But there were already 700,000 dead. It took several months for all the victims to be burned. During that time, for many miles around Treblinka, the flames could be seen, and the terrible smell of burning bodies filled the air.

Wiping out the traces

While the women and children from the first 20 cars of a transport, and then the men, were being killed in the gas chambers, the permanent prisoners sorted through all their belongings. All identification had to be removed. The Jewish stars that the Nazis had ordered the Jews to wear were ripped off the clothing. The names were taken off their suitcases. The Nazis were sending the belongings of the dead to Germany. No one was to know where they came from. Huge mounds of clothing and shoes were gathered in a large open area. The money, gold, jewelry, and other valuables that the Jews had handed over in return for a "receipt" were now the property of the Nazis. Their identification papers, passports, and birth certificates were burned. So were photographs and letters. The Nazis wanted no trace of their victims to survive.

Meanwhile, the next 20 cars of the train, which had been parked farther away, were brought to the camp. The whole process was repeated.

When Treblinka was operating at its peak, the entire process—from the arrival of a train to the time that people entered the gas chamber—took less than two hours.

The "permanent" prisoners of the death camps

At first, the Nazis killed everyone who arrived on a train before the next one arrived. Some of the Jewish men from each transport were forced to clean the cars and sort the prisoners' possessions before being sent to the gas chambers themselves.

After a while, however, the Nazis realized this was not "efficient." So they chose to keep some Jews alive to help run the killing process. That way, prisoners could be "trained" to do a particular job as each transport arrived and, with practice, could do it much faster.

There were as many as 1,300 of these prisoners in Treblinka. About 1,000 of them worked in the main part of the camp. They were divided into work groups. One group had to open the train cars and clean them. The largest group sorted the clothing and possessions of the new arrivals. Other prisoners were "barbers." Still others were sent into the woods, under heavy guard, to cut the branches that were put into the barbed wire to keep the inside of the camp hidden. Some were used as servants for the SS men.

A special group of 200 or 300 lived and worked in the separate area of the camp where the killing was done. These were the prisoners who had to separate the dead bodies and take them to the burial pits.

All the "permanent" prisoners understood that they had been spared from death only for a short time. If any of them became sick or too weak to work fast enough, they were killed immediately and replaced by men from the next transport. Their work was exhausting; guards constantly screamed at them to work faster and whipped them for "loafing." The Nazis made "selections" of who should die two or three times a day, at each roll call. The men whose names were called would be taken to the "infirmary" and shot.

The prisoners knew that when the last train had arrived, and there were no more Jews to send to the death camps, the Nazis would not need them anymore and they would be killed. In the meantime, however, they tried to stay alive. There was always the hope that the Russian army would arrive before the Nazis could kill them all. Perhaps they could escape when they were outside the camp, cutting down trees. Some did succeed in escaping by hiding in the trains that left the camps loaded with piles of clothing taken from the dead. They made plans to overpower their guards, take their weapons, and fight their way to freedom. In Sobibór and Treblinka, prisoners did fight the Nazis, and, although most were killed, some escaped. (See "The Treblinka Uprising" box on p. 237.)

Women inmates sort through a pile of shoes from those who were gassed. The Nazis sent their victims' belongings to Germany.

The price of survival

The suffering of the "permanent" prisoners of Treblinka, Belzec, and Sobibór was not just physical. They had to endure

Saving a Friend's Life

Samuel Willenberg, one of the few survivors of Treblinka, describes what happened when his boyhood friend Alfred Boehm became ill. A typhus epidemic, a serious bacterial disease transmitted usually by body lice, was raging through the camp, and more than half the "permanent" prisoners had died—most shot when they became too weak to work:

> At daybreak, I dragged him out of bed by force and, struggling, dressed him and laced his boots. Hesitantly, supported by me, he made it to the roll call. I stood behind him, as the fifth man in the row, supporting him from time to time and holding his body erect. After roll call ... I took Alfred back to the hut and placed him under a bed which had already been made. No one could see that a man was concealed there. I covered him carefully with blankets and left only a small hole to admit some air.

> For five days, Willenberg dragged his friend to the roll calls and hid him during the day. During one roll call, when he was afraid an SS man would notice how sick Boehm looked, Willenberg and another prisoner staged a fight. "I grabbed Alfred's head, as if beating him, and supported him with my shoulder." The other prisoner held Alfred from behind. The SS man walked away.

> Alfred Boehm recovered from typhus, but he was killed in the Treblinka uprising on August 2, 1943. (See box on p. 237.)

agony beyond the beatings, disease, and constant threat of death. They had arrived on the trains with their parents, wives, children, friends, and neighbors. All were now dead. In many cases, they had seen their loved ones marched off to be killed but were helpless to do anything. Perhaps even worse, their own survival depended on how well they worked at their jobs helping the Nazis kill more Jews.

Their survival depended on the death transports in another way too. The new arrivals often brought food with them, for their trip "to the east." The prisoners who sorted through their clothing took this food for themselves and

The Treblinka Uprising

A small group of Treblinka prisoners began to plan an uprising in early 1943. Eventually, one of the prisoners was able to make a copy of the key to the storeroom where the guards kept their weapons. On the day of the uprising, the prisoners secured about a dozen rifles and hand grenades and some pistols without being noticed. Gasoline was sprayed on the camp's wooden buildings by a prisoner who pretended to be disinfecting them. Wire cutters were hidden.

But the uprising did not go as the prisoners planned. The reasons are not completely clear, but according to one version of events, a little while before the time planned for the attack one of the prisoners was searched by an SS man. He had money on him that he intended to use after escaping. The other prisoners were afraid he would be tortured and reveal the plan. So, although they were not ready—and some of the weapons had not been distributed—they shot the SS man.

This set off the uprising. The prisoners set almost the entire camp on fire and fought the Nazis and Ukrainian guards, who fired on them from the watchtower. About 400 Jews were killed, and another hundred were captured inside the camp. Three or four hundred were able to escape. Most of them were quickly killed or captured by patrols. But about 150 to 200 succeeded in getting away. Many were killed fighting German troops before the war finally ended. Between 40 and 70, including Samuel Willenberg, survived. (See box on p. 236.)

their fellow prisoners. This meant that the prisoners often had more and better food than when they had been starving in the ghettos before being sent to the camp. In addition, they could have warm clothes and boots for the winter. Sometimes they even found money hidden in the clothing of the new arrivals. Although the punishment for this was death, the brave ones took the money and used it to bribe the Ukrainian guards in exchange for food.

The Nazis had set up a system where the survival of these few Jews depended on the deaths of thousands of others. As long as the trains arrived, the "permanent" prisoners were needed and might be allowed to live for a while longer.

The end of Operation Reinhard

By the time of the Treblinka uprising (see p. 237) and a similar uprising in Sobibór in October 1943, the work of the three camps of Operation Reinhard was almost done. Belzec had already been shut down. There were no more transports. The Jews of Poland were dead. Those that remained were in hiding. Jews from other parts of Europe were now being sent to Auschwitz.

The burned ruins of Treblinka were dismantled in the fall of 1943. At each camp, the fences and watchtowers were taken down. The ground was plowed over. A crop was planted. The Nazis wanted the camps, like their victims, to disappear without a trace.

In a little over a year of operation, 7,800 railroad cars had arrived at Treblinka. They arrived full of terrified human beings. They left completely empty or with only the clothes of the dead.

9

Auschwitz

T he name "Auschwitz" has become virtually synonymous with the Holocaust. Its
mere mention conjures up horrific visions of
Nazi brutality. Auschwitz is the German name
for a small town in southwestern Poland. (In
Polish, the town is called Oswiecim.) There,
the Nazis built the largest slave-labor camp
and the largest murder camp ever known. In
this place alone, they killed more than 10,000
Russian prisoners of war, over 15,000 Roma
(Gypsies), tens of thousands of Poles (though
no one knows the exact number), and more
than 1,000,000 Jews.

In the years since World War II (1939–45),
as the almost unbelievable scale of the Holocaust has been revealed, Auschwitz has become
a symbol of the darkest side of humanity—
human beings willfully destroying other
human beings. In his book *The Kingdom of
Auschwitz*, Otto Friedrich was not speaking

only of the Nazis or the Holocaust when he said of the camp: "This was the worst that has ever happened."

The concentration camp

Although the people who lived there were Poles, not Germans, the area around Auschwitz was made part of Germany when the German army conquered Poland in 1939 at the beginning of World War II. It was swampy and damp around Auschwitz, with few sources of fresh water. Mosquitos posed a serious problem in warm weather. It was also very cold in the winter.

But Auschwitz offered certain advantages to the Nazis. It was situated in the middle of nowhere yet had good railroad connections. There was also an old Polish army base located there, and the abandoned barracks would provide housing for the Nazis' victims.

In the spring of 1940, the Nazis opened a concentration camp. Concentration camps had existed in Germany since the Nazi Party had taken power. These camps served as prisons for the Nazis' opponents. The camps were run by the SS (the initials for *Schutzstaffel*), the party's black-uniformed "security" troops. Prisoners worked endless hours at jobs like quarrying rocks out of the ground. They were underfed, constantly threatened, frequently whipped or otherwise beaten as punishment for breaking minor rules, and could be executed without trial.

The first inmates of Auschwitz were Polish political prisoners—Poles who had been members of anti-Nazi political parties before the war or who had done something to oppose the German occupiers of their country. In May 1940, Rudolph Höss, an SS man who had earlier commanded Sachsenhausen, a concentration camp in Germany, was appointed the commandant (commander) of Auschwitz.

The *kapos*

A group of prisoners from Sachsenhausen was also sent to Auschwitz. These men were ordinary criminals, robbers and burglars who had been sent to concentration camps instead of prison. The criminals from Sachsenhausen went to Auschwitz to take charge of the other prisoners. They were called *kapos* and had special privileges, such as more and bet-

*Portrait of an SS
concentration camp
guard and his dog.*

ter food and a private room in the barracks. They supervised
the barracks and the workgangs. They also served as spies for
the SS, informing on the political prisoners. The *kapos* were
often as cruel as the SS officers, punishing the other prisoners with beatings. They divided the food unfairly to reward
their friends and assigned the hardest work to those who
opposed them.

This system, with the most brutal and criminal prisoners put in charge of others, was a feature of Auschwitz that
continued even after the camp had expanded to many times
its original size. Eventually, other types of prisoners became
kapos, including Jews. Although most *kapos* were hated, some
tried their best to protect the other prisoners and became
leaders in figuring out ways to survive. But these were the
exceptions. Although the *kapos* had a great deal of power
compared to other prisoners, they were still prisoners themselves, completely at the mercy of the Nazis.

Rudolph Höss

Rudolph Höss grew up in a strict religious environment. His parents wanted him to be a Catholic priest. At 16, he lied about his age to join the German army and fight in World War I (1914–18). He received an Iron Cross for bravery and became an officer by the time he was 18.

Like many soldiers returning from the war, Höss could not adjust to life in the defeated German nation. He joined a paramilitary nationalist organization called the *Freikorps* or Free Corps, that put down the workers' uprisings sweeping Germany after World War I. (A paramilitary organization is a nonmilitary fighting group based on military models, nationalism is an extreme loyalty to one's country.) The Free Corps members were violently opposed to Jews, democracy, and the philosophies of socialism and communism. (Democracy is a government by the people. Socialism is a political and economic system based on government control of the production and distribution of goods. Communism is a political and economic theory advocating the formation of a classless society through the communal, or group, ownership of all property.) The Nazis' first military organization, the *Sturmabteilungen,* or SA, or storm troopers, was full of Free Corps veterans. (See Chapter 1, p. 160.)

In 1922, Höss heard Adolf Hitler speak in Munich and joined the Nazi Party, which was still very small. At the same time, he gave up his affiliation with the Catholic Church. The next year, Höss and some other Free Corps men beat one of their former comrades to death because they thought he was a police informant. Höss was sentenced to ten years in prison for his part in the crime but was released after serving half his time.

When Hitler came to power in 1933, Höss joined the *Schutzstaffel,* or SS, the arm of the SA in charge of destroying the Jews, and served at Dachau, the first concentration camp. He then worked at the German concentration camp Sachsenhausen before being chosen as commandant of Auschwitz.

After World War II, Höss was a witness at the trial of the main Nazi leaders. His testimony then, and later at his own trial, was different than that of almost any other Nazi. He did not try to avoid answering questions. He openly admitted what had happened at Auschwitz and explained it in detail. He also described the part played by other Nazis.

At the same time, however, he did not appear to understand the horror of his crimes. Historians note that he did not seem sorry, remorseful, or even apologetic. Nor did he seem like a fanatical Nazi who committed these crimes because he hated Jews. His attitude was quite simple: he had carried out his job to the best of his abilities. His job happened to be the organization of mass murder.

In his autobiography, *Commandant of Auschwitz,* written while he waited to be executed, Höss recalled with fondness his life at Auschwitz and the beautiful rose garden that his wife had planted there. Only a few hundred yards from the house where his wife gardened and his children played was Block 11, where the Gestapo (an abbreviation for *Geheime Staatspolizei,* or the Nazi secret police) tortured prisoners, and Block 10, where SS doctors performed horrible "medical" experiments on them. A few hundred yards in a different direction was gas chamber and crematorium number 1.

Höss was hanged at Auschwitz in 1947.

The expansion of Auschwitz

During 1940, a large area of the countryside around Auschwitz was taken over by the camp. Seven small villages were emptied of their people. The territory of the camp was about 15.5 square miles.

By the beginning of March 1941, 11,000 prisoners had been through Auschwitz, but many were already dead. Prisoners never received enough to eat, especially men doing heavy physical labor. The barracks were unheated, and the prisoners were not given warm clothing. In addition, the primitive sanitation conditions and filthy drinking water contributed to the spread of disease among the inmates. All of these things led to poor health, exhaustion, and eventual death for some of the victims of Auschwitz.

Many other prisoners of Auschwitz were executed by the Nazis. Some died in the building called "Block 11," where the Gestapo (the *Geheime Staatspolizei,* the German secret police)

Polish children imprisoned in the Auschwitz concentration camp look out from behind the barbed-wire fence. Auschwitz was the Nazis' largest slave-labor and murder camp.

Block 11

If a prisoner did not talk when he was questioned by the Gestapo, he was beaten. If he still did not reveal what the German secret police wanted to know, he was tortured. Prisoners had their fingernails slowly pulled out with pliers. They were tied to a metal bar by the wrists and ankles and swung around while being beaten with a club. When they were taken out of this torture contraption—on a stretcher—their faces and bodies were so badly damaged that they could not be recognized.

Prisoners knew that if they still did not talk, they might be placed in "standing cells." These were small boxes that provided only enough room to stand up. The prisoner was left to stand in one of these boxes, without being fed, sometimes for two or three weeks, until starving to death.

"questioned" prisoners suspected of planning to escape or of organizing resistance to the Nazi Party. The Gestapo tortured these prisoners to make them give up the names of other prisoners who were helping them. Still others were shot at the "wall of death," a wall of black cork with sand in front of it to soak up the blood of the bullet-ridden bodies.

Himmler's visit

On March 1, 1941, Auschwitz was inspected by Heinrich Himmler. Himmler was the head of the SS and of the Gestapo. This meant he was in charge of the terror machinery of both the Nazi Party and of the German government under Adolf Hitler. He was probably the second most powerful person in Germany, after Hitler himself.

Himmler was accompanied on his visit by high officials of I. G. Farben, the giant German chemical company. He ordered a vast expansion of Auschwitz. The concentration camp itself was to grow so that it could hold 30,000 prisoners. This section became known as Auschwitz I.

Himmler also ordered the building of a second camp about two miles away. It was to hold 100,000 prisoners. Soon,

this number was raised to 200,000. This immense camp would be Auschwitz II, also known as *Birkenau,* from the German word for "birch trees."

In addition, there would be a third camp, Auschwitz III, in the nearby village of Monowitz. There, I. G. Farben would build a factory to make artificial rubber to supply tires for the trucks of the German army. A plant would be constructed to convert coal into oil. Himmler would supply the company with 10,000 prisoners to work in the factory.

Auschwitz and the "Final Solution"

Himmler's plan was not just to make Auschwitz a much larger concentration camp. Auschwitz was to be the key center for the destruction of the Jews of Europe. At the time of Himmler's visit in March 1941, the German armies had conquered most of Europe up to the Soviet border. Hitler intended for Germany to dominate this territory forever.

Heinrich Himmler (second from the left), head of the SS (the Nazis' security force) and the Gestapo (the German secret police), on an inspection of Auschwitz in 1942.

In addition, as Himmler knew, Hitler was planning to invade the Soviet Union (Russia). He wanted to take control of the Soviet Union's entire western section *and* lay claim to the countries the Soviet Union ruled, such as Ukraine and Belarussia (White Russia). If he could succeed in reaching this goal, almost all the Jews of Europe would be in areas controlled by Nazi Germany.

But there was an ironic twist to these plans for territorial expansion. Ever since their rise to power, the Nazis had been forcing Jews out of Germany. With the victories of the German army, though, most of these Jews would again be in German-controlled territory. The new "solution" was to kill them. The Nazis called it the "Final Solution."

The first mass killings

Three months after Himmler's visit to Auschwitz, the German armies invaded the Soviet Union and began to execute their plans for the mass murder of the Jewish people. (See Chapter 7.) While this was happening, the Nazis conducted an experiment at Auschwitz. In September 1941, they took 250 Polish prisoners from the camp hospital to the Gestapo's Block 11. They also rounded up 600 Russian prisoners of war. These prisoners were chosen because they were Jewish or because they were Communists.

In a cellar of Block 11, all of these prisoners were gassed to death. The gas used was called Zyklon B, a brand name for a powerful disinfectant—hydrogen cyanide—used to kill lice. Anyone who handled it had to wear a gas mask. Anyone who breathed it for any length of time would die.

Rudolph Höss, the Auschwitz commander, would later brag about the efficiency of Zyklon B. It was faster-acting and therefore far more effective than carbon monoxide, the gas used at the other death camps that would soon be operating in Poland. (See Chapter 8.) Höss was proud that Auschwitz, the camp under his command, was the Nazis' top-rated killing place. (See box on p. 242 for a discussion of Höss's life.)

Beginning of the death camps

Soon a room in the crematorium at Auschwitz was converted into a gas chamber. The crematorium had originally been built to burn the bodies of prisoners who were executed or who died from "natural" causes. The terrible conditions at Auschwitz almost ensured that a significant number of prisoners would die there every day without being gassed.

The Nazis used their new gas chamber to kill hundreds of Russian prisoners of war. Later, transport trains filled with Jews began to arrive at Auschwitz. Sometimes, every person on a train was taken immediately to the gas chamber and killed.

But this first gas chamber at Auschwitz was not big enough to suit the Nazis' needs; in addition, the crematorium kept breaking down. Furthermore, the chamber was situated in the main camp, which made it difficult to conceal what was happening within its walls. The killing would have to be moved to the new camp, Birkenau.

Birkenau

In October 1941, a month after the gassing of 850 men in Block 11, the prisoners began to build Auschwitz II or Birkenau. It was far bigger than any other concentration camp. Row after row of wooden barracks were built to hold the inmates. Prisoners would be crammed into these buildings, sleeping on narrow planks, or bunks, arranged three tiers high. Three men slept on each plank; there was so little space for the men that if one of them died during the night, it was impossible to move his body until the morning. The sanitary facilities were completely inadequate for so many prisoners, and a horrible stench from human waste, filth, and death was a permanent feature of the camp.

On the grounds of Birkenau were two small cottages surrounded by woods. These had been the homes of Polish farmers. Each was far enough from the barracks to insure privacy. One of these cottages was made of red brick and had a tile roof. The Nazis called it Bunker 1, but the prisoners called it "the little red house." The other had plastered walls and a thatched roof. It was Bunker 2, nicknamed "the little white house" by the prisoners.

At the beginning of 1942, the Nazis bricked up the windows of these cottages and sealed the doors so no air could get in or out. These were the new gas chambers. Thousands and thousands of people eventually died in them. But like

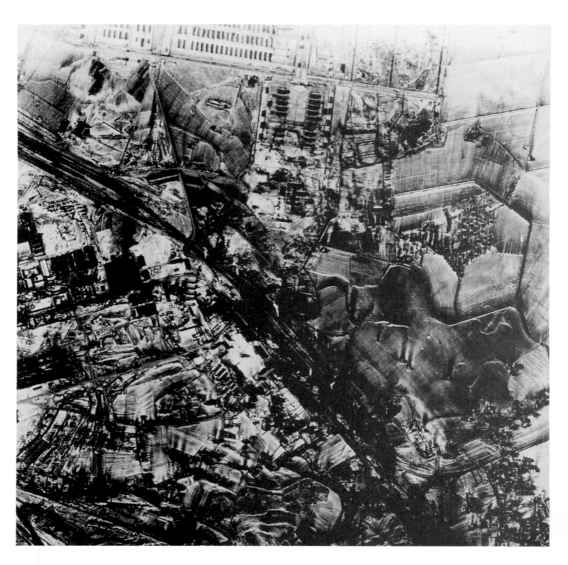

An aerial photograph of the Auschwitz area showing the Birkenau camp taken by the Allies in 1944.

Crematorium I, the original crematoria at Auschwitz I, they could not handle the enormous number of victims that the Nazis intended to kill at Auschwitz.

The two cottages had no ventilation equipment, so after a gassing it took a long time for the rooms to be cleared of Zyklon B fumes. After people were gassed in the evening, it was necessary to open the doors all night before the bodies could be removed. This meant the gas chambers could not be used continuously. In addition, the bodies had to be moved to large pits where they were buried. The two cottages proved

A door to a gas chamber in Auschwitz. The note reads: "Harmful gas! Entering endangers your life."

to be only temporary answers to the problem of how to kill more people in one place than had ever been killed before. But the Nazis had already decided on a still more efficient way of destroying the Jews.

The death factory

In October 1941, at the time that construction of Birkenau began, the SS ordered the erection of four special buildings on the site. German engineering and construction companies were hired to design and build them, although the actual labor was performed by prisoners. The work on these buildings went on frantically 24 hours a day, but it took until the spring of 1943 to complete them.

The buildings were crematoria, each one holding furnaces designed to burn bodies. The buildings called crematoria IV and V were over 100 yards long and about 40 feet wide. Crematoria II and III were smaller because they also had underground rooms. A tall brick chimney rose high above each structure.

But unlike crematorium I, the four new crematoria were not designed to burn the bodies of prisoners who had died from malnutrition, exhaustion, or the diseases that swept through the concentration camp. Instead, they were conceived as a crucial mechanism in the plan to bring about the Final Solution.

Part of each building housed a large gas chamber. These too had been carefully planned by experts. In each crematorium building, 2,000 people could be gassed to death at one time. The furnaces of the crematoria would then burn their bodies.

In crematoria II and III, the gas chambers were located in the basement. A freight elevator connected them with the furnaces on the ground floor. The doors to the elevator joining both levels were designed to open automatically. In contrast to Treblinka and the other death camps, then, there was no need to take the bodies of the victims from the gas chambers to open pits where they would be buried. (See Chapter 8 for a description of Treblinka and other death camps.)

The transports

The first new prisoners were Jews from the area around Auschwitz. In March 1942, transports of Jews from Slovakia began. Then came the first transports from distant France. That summer, trains carried Jews across Europe from France, Belgium, and Holland to Auschwitz. The trains all had the same official orders: "This transport conforms to the standing orders and should be included in the special operation." The "special operation" was the murder of the Jews of Europe. The "standing orders" were to kill them.

Prisoners would be transported to Auschwitz for two-and-a-half more years from all over Nazi-controlled Europe.

The Jews of Europe

Auschwitz was the main killing center for much of Nazi-occupied Europe. A recent study by Franciszek Piper, the chief historian of the official Auschwitz museum, attempts to trace the home countries of the Jews deported to Auschwitz. Although Piper's numbers cannot be exact, most experts agree that they are probably very close:

Hungary	438,000
Poland	300,000
France	69,000
Holland	60,000
Greece	55,000
Bohemia and Moravia (the Czech Republic today)	46,000
Slovakia	27,000
Belgium	25,000
Germany and Austria	23,000
Yugoslavia	10,000
Italy	7,500
Norway	690

Piper was not able to trace the original home of about 34,000 Jews because, in most cases, they were sent to Auschwitz from other concentration camps.

But not all Jews were sent to Auschwitz. For example, Jews living in the territory that Germany captured from the Soviet Union were usually killed by special SS units called *Einsatzgruppen* without being sent to camps. (The SS was the Nazi group charged with destroying the Jews. See pp. 186–88 for a discussion of the *Einsatzgruppen*.) And although the Jews who lived in the part of Romania that was taken over by Hungary during World War II did go to Auschwitz, other Romanian Jews did not.

In other countries, only a minority of the Jews who were killed met their deaths at Auschwitz. Almost 200,000 German and Austrian Jews were killed by the Nazis, but only 23,000 were sent to Auschwitz. And, although about 300,000 Polish Jews died in Auschwitz, the Nazis killed ten times that number, most of them in other camps.

In the late summer of 1942, the Jews of Croatia were sent there, then more from Holland arrived. Half the small Jewish population of Norway reached Auschwitz in November. In February 1943, the transports brought the last Jews of Berlin, the capital of Nazi Germany. The next month the Jews of Greece arrived. In the fall and winter, the Italian Jews were funneled in. Then, in the spring of 1944, the Nazis sent hundreds of thousands of Hungarian Jews to Auschwitz. Finally, by August, 70,000 Jews from Lódz (the last Polish ghetto), along with the final transport of French Jews, were loaded up and sent to their deaths at Auschwitz—even while the American and British armies were driving the Germans from France.

Hungarian Jewish women, separated from the men, await "selection" on a ramp at Auschwitz in May 1944.

The railroad tracks carried the Jewish passengers right into Birkenau. When they reached the camp, the prisoners were already exhausted. Many had been held in transit camps in their home countries after being arrested. Then, they had traveled, packed in locked freight cars, usually with no food or water, for many days and nights. In the summer, the heat and thirst were indescribable. In the winter, the prisoners froze in the unheated railroad cars. In every transport, many died long before they reached Auschwitz.

The "selection"

When the trains stopped at Birkenau, the doors were opened and the Jews were ordered out by SS men with whips. Some children did not survive the trip. The freight cars were littered with bodies. The prisoners who were still alive at the end of the line were very hungry, frightened, drained, and absolutely horrified at some of the atrocities they had witnessed thus far. They were told to leave their suitcases or their

Luck and Chance

Sometimes, survival at Auschwitz depended on pure luck. Historian Otto Friedrich tells the story of how one man lived through it.

Sim Kessel was one of those chosen to die. Kessel was a French boxer. He had been sent to Auschwitz for being in the French resistance, the movement that opposed the Nazis. He was told to undress and stood naked, with the others, waiting in the snow.

SS men then arrived on motorcycles. Kessel saw that one of them, a corporal or sergeant, had scar tissue over his eyes and a broken nose, just like Kessel himself. Knowing he had nothing to lose, he asked the SS man whether he had been a boxer. "Yes," said the SS man, who looked at Kessel's face and recognized a fellow prizefighter.

The SS man asked Kessel where he had fought, and Kessel told him. Then, the SS man told Kessel, still naked, to hop onto the back of his motorcycle. They drove through the camp, and Kessel was taken to the hospital instead of the gas chambers.

bundles on the platform, and to stand in line and walk past two men sitting at a table. These were two SS doctors.

As each prisoner passed the table, one of the doctors waved his hand either to the left or the right, indicating which way the prisoner should go. Usually, about 90 percent were sent to the left. Children and almost all women were sent to the left, as was anyone who appeared sick or weak. All old people were sent to the left. Adult men under the age of 40 who appeared healthy had the best chance of being sent to the right.

Being sent to the right meant the doctors had decided that a prisoner was strong enough to work. Those "selected" in this way did not know it, but they had been chosen to live, at least for a while. Those sent to the left would die in the gas chambers. As each train brought the Jews into Birkenau, the SS doctors went about their work of selection. Life or death

Opposite page:
Canisters of Zyklon B, a
powerful disinfectant usually
used to kill lice, and a gas
mask found after the
liberation of one of the
concentration camps. (See
pp. 246–49 and p. 256 for
discussions of the use of
Zyklon B at Auschwitz.)

might depend on how exhausted someone looked, or on the mood of the doctor that day.

The final walk

Those who were sent to the left were then marched through the camp. They were told that before going to their barracks, they would be bathed and disinfected to prevent disease. The SS men forced them forward with their whips and attack dogs. People who were too weak or sick to walk were loaded into trucks.

The exact details of what happened next tend to vary. Some of the procedures changed a little during the years that Auschwitz was operating. Additional factors might also depend on the number of people in a particular transport, and whether the train arrived during the day or at night.

This, by most accounts, is what happened to those who were sent to the buildings called Crematoria II and III.

Each of these two buildings was situated outside the fence surrounding the prisoner barracks at Birkenau. Each, in turn, was enclosed by a barbed-wire fence and numerous bushes and trees. That way, no one could see what was happening inside.

The prisoners were led down a flight of stairs to the basement. There were signs that said "To the Baths" and "To Disinfection." The permanent signs were in German, but the Nazis also posted temporary signs in the language of that day's victims.

They entered a windowless room lined with wooden benches and were told to undress. The room was 50 yards long and 8 yards wide. Above the benches were wooden hooks on which the prisoners hung their clothes. Each hook was numbered, and the victims were told to remember their number so that they could reclaim their clothes later.

When they had undressed, the prisoners were led through a narrow hall to another room; women and children usually went first. Sometimes they were given soap and a towel by the SS men. Like the signs that pointed to the "baths," this was a way of keeping the victims from realizing what was going to happen to them.

The gas chambers

This next room, the gas chamber, was smaller than the dressing room, about 30 yards by 7. It had white-washed plaster walls and metal plates on the ceiling that looked like shower heads. The SS men forced 2,000 people into this room: that's about 9 people for every square yard. Then, the SS men left and bolted the airtight door behind them. In the door was a round peephole made of thick glass protected on the inside by a metal grill.

At the command of an SS doctor, Zyklon B pellets were poured down the specially made vents into the gas chamber. These pellets turned to gas when they came in contact with air.

The people nearest the vents died first, almost immediately. The others "staggered about and began to scream and struggle for air. The screaming, however, soon changed to the death rattle and in a few minutes all lay still," noted Rudolph Höss, describing what he saw through the peephole in his memoir, *Commandant of Auschwitz*.

Other witnesses tell an even more horrible story. The pellets of Zyklon B first turned into deadly gas near the floor, then the gas rose upwards. Therefore, the children, who were shorter, died first. Sometimes, according to witnesses, the bodies were found in a pyramid. Those on top had been the strongest. They had climbed onto the dead and dying in a desperate attempt to breathe a little while longer.

The crematoria

About 30 minutes after the gas had been released, ventilation fans were turned on and the door was opened. A special squad of prisoners, wearing gas masks, dragged the bodies out. Called *Sonderkommando,* or "special commando," these prisoners were among those from earlier transports who had been "selected" to live. They removed glasses and artificial limbs from the bodies. They also cut off the hair of the women. Then, the bodies were loaded onto the elevator platform and sent up to the ground floor.

There, other members of the *Sonderkommando* removed all jewelry, such as wedding rings, from the corpses. Then, they opened the mouths of the dead and pulled out all the

The *Sonderkommando* Diaries

The men of the *Sonderkommando,* who disposed of the bodies of the Nazis' victims, had no hope of surviving the war. They knew the Nazis would never let them live to tell what they had seen. But some of them secretly wrote down their stories, sealed them in bottles or cans, then buried them among the ashes of the dead near the crematoria.

In the first fifteen years after Auschwitz was liberated, six of these hidden reports or diaries (by three different authors) were found. Each of the writers tells the story of how the Jewish community in his town was rounded up, transported to Auschwitz, and "processed" through the camp. Other eyewitness accounts are believed to have existed but are now lost. The *Sonderkommando* members make it clear in their diaries that they wrote these documents to let the world know what the Nazis had done.

gold teeth they could find. The gold would be collected, melted down, and used to help finance the German war effort. If a *Sonderkommando* worker were found to have left a gold tooth in the mouth of a victim, he was severely punished—sometimes even thrown into the furnace alive.

It took the *Sonderkommando* four hours to empty the gas chamber. Then, it took about 20 minutes for the furnace to burn the two or three corpses that had been loaded into each compartment. Sometimes, the *Sonderkommando* loaded four or five bodies into one compartment and burned the bodies longer. Crematoria II and III could each cremate about 2,500 bodies in 24 hours. Crematoria IV and V could burn as many as 1,500 bodies each in a day.

The ashes and the incompletely burned bones fell through a grill in the bottom of the furnace into a pit. The bones were ground up by members of the *Sonderkommando* and mixed with the ashes. The ashes were usually dumped into the river or ponds or used as fertilizer.

The remains of a crematorium oven at the Bergen-Belsen concentration camp. Crematorium ovens such as this were used at Auschwitz.

This was how the gas chambers could kill, and the crematoria could burn, as many as 8,000 human beings in 24 hours. Sometimes, though, even this was not enough. When large transports of Hungarian Jews were sent to Auschwitz, the crematoria could not handle the huge number of victims. The corpses had to be burned in open pits. Records dating back to the summer of 1944 indicate that the crematoria and pits together could burn 20,000 dead bodies in a single day.

"Canada"

The Nazis not only killed the prisoners of Auschwitz, they stole all of their possessions. Money from the victims was deposited in special bank accounts of the SS, the Nazi military organization charged with wiping out the Jews. Gold and silver were melted down into bars and sent to the German Central Bank.

The Jews arriving at Auschwitz had been told they would be "resettled," so many brought along clothes and household goods to establish themselves in their new homes. These things were confiscated by the Nazis and taken to warehouses. Then, the property was sorted and prepared so it could be used in the camp or shipped out for distribution to German citizens.

Eventually, dozens of buildings, including large barracks, were needed to hold all the stolen goods. Several thousand prisoners worked in these buildings, which they referred to as "Canada," probably because they thought of that country as having fabulous wealth.

The amount of property taken from the prisoners of Auschwitz is hard to believe. Even though many trainloads of loot were sent out of the camp, huge quantities of goods were found at the end of the war. As they retreated from the Soviet army, the Nazis tried to burn the "Canada" warehouses, successfully destroying 29 of them. Only 6 buildings were left standing. In these, the Soviets found 350,000 men's suits, over 800,000 women's outfits, more than 40,000 pairs of shoes, and almost 14,000 rugs.

The registered prisoners

About 1,500,500 people were sent to Auschwitz during its existence. The great majority were murdered almost immediately. Even so, a very large number, about 400,000, were officially registered as prisoners and given numbers. About half of these prisoners were Jews. They were the people, mostly healthy adult men, who had been "selected" to live by the SS doctors. Most of the rest of the registered prisoners were non-Jewish Poles.

Concentration camp prisoners, wearing uniforms with triangular badges, stand in columns under the supervision of a guard.

While their families and friends were being marched to the gas chambers, those who had survived the "selection" were "processed" by the Nazis. It took all day or all night, and during this time the prisoners remained unfed. They were brought to a yard between two barracks and told to undress. Then, they waited while each prisoner's hair was shaved off. Next, they ran naked to take cold showers, with the SS men using their whips and their dogs to hurry them. After the showers, they ran to another yard and received their camp uniforms. These were like pajamas, striped blue and white. They were also given caps, which they were required to wear at all times, and wooden clogs instead of shoes.

A colored triangle was attached to each uniform. Common criminals wore uniforms with green triangles. Political prisoners—people who had opposed the Nazis' policies—wore red. Homosexuals wore pink. Jehovah's Witnesses wore purple triangles. (Hitler had labeled members of this small Christian denomination a "degenerate race." Despite being

German descendants, Jehovah's Witnesses were considered "enemies of the state." Their fundamental beliefs, which were grounded in the teachings of the Bible, included recognizing only Jehovah as the supreme god and remaining politically neutral.) And the Jews wore yellow triangles—or sometimes two triangles to form a Jewish star.

The next step was the tattooing of a "prisoner number" on the left arm, between the wrist and the elbow.

The quarantine barracks

The prisoners were then sent to the quarantine barracks, where they were kept for a month or two. To quarantine means to isolate someone long enough to know whether they are carrying a contagious disease. The Nazis wanted to make sure the new prisoners were not harboring dangerous germs that could spread to the other prisoners or to the camp personnel. In addition, the SS guards used the quarantine time to "train" the prisoners in the routine of the concentration camp.

Inmates had to stand at roll call every day, beginning at 4:30 in the morning. The roll call always lasted several hours—and sometimes much longer. Prisoners were schooled in the Nazi method of "physical training": at each command they had to run in place, then drop down and hop like a frog, then get up and run in place again. This, too, could continue for hours. They also dug ditches and performed other physically demanding work in the quarantine area. In addition to hard labor, they were ordered to line up "correctly," to take off their caps on command, and to sing anti-Jewish songs. Then, at the end of each long and torturous day, came the evening roll call, which began at 6:30.

During all these activities, the SS and the *kapos*, the criminal prisoners who oversaw the other prisoners, scrutinized every move the prisoners made to make sure there were no "mistakes." If a prisoner did not line up according to Nazi procedures, or took too long to remove a cap, or could no longer keep up when ordered to hop, the result was a violent beating. Rules varied from day to day: an action, movement, or maneuver that was correct one day might be considered a mistake the next. It really didn't matter whether the Nazis' commands made sense. The prisoners were not supposed to think or decide, they were only supposed to obey their captors.

During the quarantine, the Nazis did everything they could to dehumanize the prisoners—to crush their spirit and make them forget that they were human beings. Inmates were viewed as nothing more than the numbers tattooed on their arms. The Nazis reminded them in every possible way that they were in a place where death was normal and expected. They wanted the prisoners to believe that the only way they might be able to live even a little while longer was by caring about no one but themselves.

It is not surprising that the stress of their imprisonment broke the will of many prisoners. There are stories, for example, of prisoners stealing food from each other. What *is* surprising, though, is the strength of many other captives. Inmates are known to have risked their lives to help others. Working together to survive, many of the victims managed to cling to their beliefs—and to their humanity.

Medical experiments

A few of the people who were "selected" by the SS doctors to live were chosen for reasons other than their potential labor value. They were chosen because the doctors wanted to use them for medical experiments.

No doctor is supposed to conduct *any* medical experiments on human beings without their consent. The experiments performed on concentration camp prisoners went far beyond this violation of accepted standards in the medical profession.

Many of the Nazi doctors' experiments caused extreme pain, and they were almost always conducted without anesthesia (painkillers) of any sort. Many of the subjects of these experiments were killed so that an autopsy could be performed on the bodies and the "success" of the experiment could be evaluated. In fact, most of the medical experiments had no serious scientific basis. They were merely attempts to "prove" Nazi ideas about race.

Robert Jay Lifton, the author of *The Nazi Doctors,* has pointed out that these experiments were only a small part of what medical doctors did at Auschwitz. Physicians were in charge of the "selections." They supervised the procedures in the gas chambers—doctors decided when to release the Zyklon B and when the victims were dead. They were also consulted on methods for burning bodies more quickly. Some critics feel that the role doctors played in the Holocaust is one of the most horrifying of all. They were trained to heal the sick, to reduce pain, and to save lives. Instead, the SS doctors used their knowledge and skills to inflict disease, to cause agony, and to commit murder.

Block 10

There were so many experimental "subjects" in Auschwitz that sometimes these test prisoners were sent elsewhere for evaluation. Children from Auschwitz, for example, were often sent to Germany to be used in testing their resistance to tuberculosis. Auschwitz was not the only place where experiments of this kind were conducted: it was only the most famous.

The main location of medical experiments at Auschwitz was Block 10. It was situated just across a courtyard from Block 11, where the Gestapo tortured prisoners. In the courtyard was the "wall of death," the black cork wall where prisoners were shot. All of the prisoners in Block 10 were Jews.

Many of the experiments involved ways to sterilize people, to alter their reproductive systems so that they could not have children. The Nazis had long been interested in preventing "inferior" or "imperfect" people, including below-standard Germans, from reproducing. Hitler had argued for this in *Mein Kampf* 20 years earlier. It was part of the Nazi idea to create a master race. (See pp. 108–14 on the euthanasia program.)

At Auschwitz, doctor Horst Schumann subjected about 1,000 young women and men of childbearing age to massive doses of X rays. They suffered great pain and many died. Approximately 200 of these victims also had their sex organs surgically removed.

Another doctor who experimented with sterilization was Claus Clauberg, who had been a fertility expert before the war, helping people who could not have children. He had personally discussed his ideas with Himmler. At Auschwitz, Clauberg injected chemicals into women's reproductive systems to find out which drugs would sterilize them. This caused agonizing pain to the women, sometimes for many weeks. Often the women's sex organs were surgically removed and sent to Berlin for further study.

Doctor Johann Kremer had been a professor of anatomy. He was interested in the effects of starvation on different organs. To further his studies, a test prisoner was placed on a dissection table, the prisoner's weight-loss history was taken, and then he or she was killed with an injection directly into the heart. Kremer immediately removed the victim's organs for study.

Josef Mengele

Doctor Josef Mengele was the most notorious of the Nazi doctors. He gained his reputation as the "Angel of Death" because of his bizarre behavior as chief of "selections" when a transport arrived. Mengele is said to have worn white gloves and hummed opera to himself while he chose who would live and who would die.

Mengele conducted experiments on dwarfs. He also subjected Roma (Gypsies) to assorted procedures. Among other things, he was probably trying to change their eye color. Mengele's best-known experiments, however, were on identical twins, including many children. He wanted to see, for example, whether each twin reacted the same way to pain. He carefully measured every part of each sibling: the shape and size of their ears, the lengths of their legs, the coloring of their skin. He tried transferring blood between them. He kept records of everything.

After the observations and studies were complete, the twins were usually killed—by an injection into the heart, sometimes performed by Mengele himself—and then dissected. Experts speculate that the twisted doctor's goal was probably to figure out how twins were produced so that more "pure Germans" could be born.

Josef Mengele, known as the "Angel of Death," performed horrific experiments that made little scientific sense.

Still, no one is truly sure what motivated him. Despite the fact that he had both a medical degree and a Ph.D., Mengele seemed to perform experiments that made little or no scientific sense.

Destruction through work

Prisoners who survived the weeks in the quarantine barracks were transferred to the regular barracks in Auschwitz I or Birkenau. The conditions they faced were intolerable.

Most alarming was the scarcity of food. Although there were official regulations regarding how much the prisoners were supposed to be fed, the Nazis usually ignored their own rules. SS men often stole the money that was supposed to be used for food purchases. Guards and *kapos* took much of the food that did get to the camp. On average, Auschwitz prisoners probably got 1,500 calories a day, but many received far less. An average adult male needs more than twice that to maintain his weight. Men working at heavy labor, as the Auschwitz prisoners did, require more than three times that many calories to produce the energy they need.

Interior view of one of the barracks of Auschwitz.

And despite the quarantining of new prisoners, the lack of sanitation in the camps meant that there were often major outbreaks of disease. Because of their poor diets and generally weakened state, the prisoners usually failed to muster enough resistance to fight off these diseases. Any germs—even the common cold—could be life-threatening. One of the most feared illnesses was typhus, a serious bacterial disease transmitted usually by body lice. In the summer of 1942, typhus killed 4,000 Auschwitz prisoners each month. There were also major outbreaks of typhoid fever, caused by drinking untreated water. (The SS men and the employees of the German companies building Birkenau were given free bottled water to drink.)

The high death rate from the combination of disease, malnutrition, and exhaustion was not an accident. It was the goal. As part of the Final Solution, the Nazis had decided that a small number of Jews would not be killed immediately in the gas chambers. Instead they would be made to work until they died. This was called "destruction through work."

The Nazis secretly discussed how this policy should work. In September 1942, Joseph Goebbels, one of the top Nazi officials, told a meeting in Berlin that "destruction through work" should apply to all Jews and Gypsies in concentration camps, to Poles who were sentenced to more than three years, and to Germans and Czechs sentenced to life in prison. "The idea of exterminating them by labor is best," he said. In addition, individuals outside these categories could be included, depending on the specific case.

On the gate at Auschwitz, as at other concentration camps, was the slogan *"Arbeit Macht Frei"*—"Work makes you free." But the real purpose of work at Auschwitz was not freedom. It was death.

Inside the camps

Many prisoners were needed to keep the concentration camps running. Some worked on the construction of new

View of the entrance to the main camp of Auschwitz. The gate bears the motto "Arbeit Macht Frei" ("Work makes you free").

An Auschwitz warehouse filled with sacks of human hair used to make thread.

buildings as Birkenau expanded. Others worked in "Canada," the storehouses where the loot of the dead was sorted and prepared. Some worked on farms inside the camp, where the Nazis experimented with ways to grow new crops; or as barbers, who shaved the new prisoners; or as kitchen help—a very desirable job, because it was possible to steal extra food. Others were assigned to the *Sonderkommando:* their job was to empty the gas chambers and dispose of the bodies.

Many other prisoners worked outside the electrified fences of Auschwitz and Birkenau but returned each night. They would be marched under heavy guard to their workplaces, sometimes several miles, regardless of the weather, before beginning an 11- or 12-hour shift of work. Among these workers were members of the "shoe commando," women prisoners who worked in a hut outside the camp, separating parts of shoes so the leather or the soles could be reused. In a second hut, as one prisoner remembered, "thousands and thousands of dusty, decaying, moldy shoes were crammed together in the pitch dark." These were the shoes of the murdered Jews. Yet another "commando" consisted of women who made thread from the hair of the female prisoners whose heads had been shaved.

In all these jobs, the half-starved prisoners were expected to work at full speed, without ever taking a break except for lunch, which was usually a watery soup. They still had their long roll calls each morning and night. They were not given enough time to sleep. Sunday was supposed to be a rest day, but they were often forced to do "physical training," or "sport," as the Nazis called it. Sometimes, Sundays were used for special jobs like moving bricks from one part of the camp to another.

If prisoners did not work fast enough, they were beaten. If they broke a camp rule, they were punished by whipping. Serious violations were punishable by death. Finally, inmates who became too sick or too tired to work were "selected" for the gas chambers.

The family camps

Almost all registered prisoners in Auschwitz and Birkenau were segregated by gender; no contact between men and women was allowed. A special women's camp was set up in Birkenau, with SS women in charge. Hardly any children lived in the Auschwitz camps because children were usually "selected" for death when a transport arrived. A few young people survived by convincing the SS doctors that they were older than they looked. Other children, especially twins, were spared immediate death in the gas chambers because Mengele had chosen them for his medical experiments.

For a while, however, there were two "family camps" set up inside Auschwitz. In these camps, whole families were allowed to live together. The Nazis had special reasons to create each of these special camps.

The Jewish family camp

One of these camps was established in September 1943. The prisoners chosen for it came from the Theresienstadt "model ghetto" in what is now the Czech Republic.

Theresienstadt was a camp created for German Jews whom the Nazis, for various reasons, treated more favorably

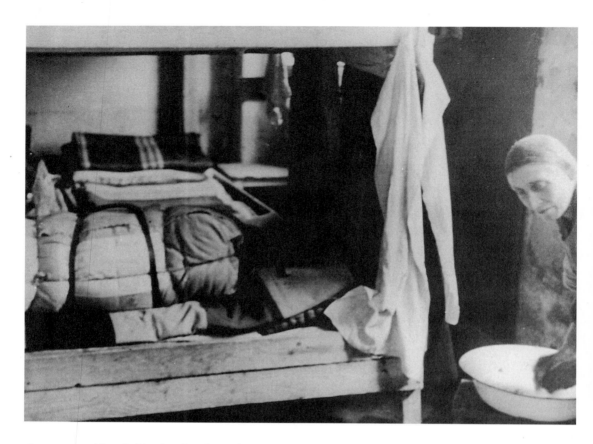

A woman washing clothing in a barracks at Theresienstadt. Theresienstadt, a "model ghetto," was the only concentration camp ever opened to outside inspectors.

than the others. Some were famous artists or writers or leaders of the Jewish community. The conditions at Theresienstadt were among the best in the concentration camp system. The Nazis held up this special camp as a model—they used it to try to convince people that they treated the Jews well. They even made films featuring Theresienstadt; it was the only camp to be inspected by the International Red Cross, an organization concerned with ending human suffering and promoting public health. (See box on Theresienstadt on p. 294.)

The Red Cross inspection led to the establishment of a family camp at Auschwitz. Rumors that Jews were being murdered in Auschwitz and Birkenau were spreading, and the Red Cross wanted to inspect Birkenau. So the Nazis sent a transport of 5,000 people from Theresienstadt to Auschwitz. When the transport arrived, there was no "selection." Instead, families remained together in barracks in a special section of the camp. They were not given prison uniforms, and their heads were not shaved.

However, this was not really a "model ghetto" like Theresienstadt. The dietary and sanitary conditions were similar to the rest of Auschwitz. About one out of every five prisoners in the family camp died within six months.

A second transport of 5,000 more people arrived from Theresienstadt three months later, in December 1943.

Postcards from the dead

On March 7, 1944, the people in the family camp were given postcards by the Nazis. The prisoners had to address the postcards to relatives, including those in Theresienstadt. They were instructed to write that they were in good health and being treated well. These postcards were predated March 25—more than two weeks after they were written.

But on the night of March 7, every survivor of the first transport was taken out of the family camp and sent to the gas chambers. There was no "selection." Even those who were healthy and could work were killed. They had been in Auschwitz exactly six months.

Two more transports arrived from Theresienstadt. A special code was written by their names: SB6. The letters stood for the German words for "special handling" or "special treatment." The number "6" meant six months. SB6 meant that they were to be killed six months after their arrival.

Meanwhile, representatives of the International Red Cross inspected Theresienstadt on June 23, 1944, and were scheduled to stop at Birkenau after that. But the Nazis convinced them that this second stop was not necessary. Perhaps the Red Cross inspectors were shown the postcards from the people in the family camp.

By July, the people who had arrived at Auschwitz in the December transport were taken from the family camp and sent to the gas chambers. Their six months were up. At the same time, those who had come in the later transports were "selected." Those able to work were sent to other barracks in Auschwitz or Birkenau. The others, including the children, were gassed. It was the end of the Jewish family camp.

Roma (or "Gypsies") in Auschwitz

The other family camp at Auschwitz was set up for Gypsies, who prefer to be called Roma. Nazi policy toward the

A close-up of a Roma (Gypsy) couple sitting in an open area in a concentration camp.

Roma was highly inconsistent. Sometimes they were treated as badly as the Jews; at other times, and in some parts of Nazi-controlled Europe, they were left alone. (See Chapter 5, p. 139.)

The Nazis ordered German Roma to Auschwitz early in 1943; the first transport reached the camp on February 26. Over the next few months, transports of Roma arrived from various areas of Europe. By the end of 1943, almost 19,000 Roma had reached Auschwitz.

As early as March, when they were first arriving, 1,700 Roma who were ill with typhoid fever were sent to the gas chambers. Another 1,000 sick people were murdered at the end of May. Although some Roma were transferred to the regular labor camps at Auschwitz and to other concentration camps, most lived in family units in the special Gypsy camp. No one is sure why the Nazis allowed this.

Another mystery concerns the events of May 17, 1944. On that day, the SS surrounded the Roma camp and prepared to lead all of its occupants to the gas chambers. The Roma, who had been warned—apparently by the German commander of the Roma camp—were waiting with iron pipes and knives. The SS men, who could easily have shot down all the Roma, were ordered to retreat instead.

A week later, about 1,500 of the Roma were transferred from the family camp to the main camps, where they were assigned to work details. In August, another 1,400 were "selected" for work, and the rest of the people in the camp, including the children, were killed in the gas chambers.

About 6,500 Roma died in the gas chambers at Auschwitz. Another 10,000 died from disease and hunger.

Auschwitz III: The slave-labor system

One of the reasons for Himmler's decision to expand Auschwitz was to enable I. G. Farben, the huge chemical company, to build a factory there using slave labor. The I. G. Farben factory at Monowitz, called Auschwitz III, was built by Auschwitz prisoners. In addition to the usual problems they faced—malnutrition, disease, and beatings among them— the prisoners were forced to work on a large construction site without any safety equipment. It is estimated that 25,000 prisoners died while building the factory.

Monowitz was only one of the 25 to 50 sub-camps of Auschwitz, some of them located as far as 50 miles away from the main camp. (The number depends on whether certain camps are counted separately or as parts of the same sub-camp.) Prisoners were sent to work in steel factories, a cement plant, a shoe factory, and in coal mines. In one plant, opened by the Krupp steel company, prisoners made fuses for bombs.

The Nazis maintained their philosophy of "destruction through work" (meaning they would work some prisoners to death) throughout the rest of the war, so the horrendous conditions under which the Auschwitz captives labored came as no surprise. But some jobs were worse than others. Being stationed in the coal mine at Jaworzno, for instance, was considered the same as a death sentence. Very few prisoners had experience as miners, so they were given jobs that required intense physical labor and no skill. Prisoners loaded coal onto carts and hauled it around. They worked in sweltering heat with poor ventilation inside the mine, often on their hands and knees. Desperate for water, they sometimes drank their own urine. They had no hard hats, boots, or other safety equipment. This, combined with their inexperience at such dangerous work, guaranteed that there would be serious injuries every day.

Auschwitz prisoners on mining duty were required to produce as much coal as regular miners, but none of the prisoners received anywhere near enough food to do this kind of work. The Jewish prisoners were only allowed half as much food as German prisoners.

Jews made up the great majority of inmates in all the sub-camps. At Jaworzno, for example, about 80 percent of the slave laborers were Jews. In some sub-camps, the percentage was higher. Those who could not keep up were sent back to Auschwitz to be gassed. SS doctors from Auschwitz made inspections of the sub-camps and "selected" those workers who would die.

The SS, not the workers, were paid for this slave labor. For instance, I. G. Farben is said to have paid the SS one dollar a day for each skilled worker and 75 cents a day for unskilled workers. Children brought the SS about 40 cents a day. But the Nazis spent less than 35 cents a day to maintain each prisoner. By 1944, 37,000 prisoners (out of a total of 105,000 registered prisoners) worked for private companies as slave laborers. Eleven thousand of these worked for I. G. Farben.

Other prisoners worked for companies owned by the SS itself. One of these companies was among the largest brick producers in Germany. In fact, the SS often based the location of a new concentration camp on its proximity (closeness) to deposits of clay that could be used for making bricks. That way, the SS-owned company would always have enough workers—workers who did not have to be paid, who could not quit, and who could be forced to work under subhuman conditions.

Uprising

The prisoners who made up the *Sonderkommando* had the most gruesome jobs. Day after day they had to witness the results of the gassings and then dispose of the bodies. As the summer of 1944 ended, the Nazis were almost finished

Escape from Auschwitz

Prisoners tried to escape from Auschwitz throughout its history. Even an escape by one or two prisoners—one that was not discovered immediately—was very difficult to make. The camp was surrounded by a high-voltage electrified fence. Anyone who approached the area near the fence was shot without warning by the SS guards sitting above in high watchtowers. Outside the fence was a large security area, about 15 square miles; it was patrolled by the SS and closed to civilians.

As soon as an escape was discovered, the SS searched every likely hiding place in the security zone around the camp. They sent men into the watchtowers scattered in this large area. Dogs were used to hunt down the prisoners.

A successful escape usually required careful preparation and help from secret Polish organizations fighting the Nazis, called the underground, outside the camp. That way escaped prisoners could be given civilian clothes, wigs to hide their shaved heads, and false identification papers. They could be hidden and fed until they were strong enough to travel. Several times, Auschwitz prisoners escaped by wearing stolen SS uniforms and walking right through the gate.

The Nazis continued to hunt for escaped prisoners, even if they had gotten far from the camp. They sent their names and serial numbers—which were tattooed on the prisoners' arms—to every police station and border patrol.

Prisoners who were captured after escaping were brought back to Auschwitz, tortured by the Gestapo to make them reveal who had helped them, and then hanged in front of the assembled prisoners. Many times, the Nazis also executed other prisoners in the same barracks or work squad. That way, prisoners who were thinking of escaping would know that even if they succeeded their fellow prisoners would die because of them.

---

with the mass killing of the Hungarian Jews. The *Sonderkommando* knew that when their work was done, they themselves would be killed. There was no chance that the Nazis would allow them—having seen so much—to leave Auschwitz alive.

The *Sonderkommando* men managed to have explosive powder smuggled to them from one of the slave-labor factories where Auschwitz prisoners worked. A few of the women in the factory, led by a young woman named Róza Robota, were able to get explosives to the *Sonderkommando* a little at a time. On October 7, 1944, the members of the *Sonderkommando* blew up Crematorium IV and attempted to escape. Then, the *Sonderkommando* in Crematorium II overwhelmed

Róza Robota, a prisoner who worked in an Auschwitz factory, managed to smuggle explosives to the Sonderkommando, *aiding in their uprising. She was arrested and hanged.*

the German *kapo* and an SS officer and threw them—alive—into the furnace. They too tried to break out of the camp.

The Nazis sent hundreds of SS guards after the escaped *Sonderkommando*. Many of them were trapped inside a barn within the camp. The SS set it on fire and shot the prisoners as they tried to get out. About 250 *Sonderkommando* were killed, and another 200 were executed soon after. Three SS men were killed and a dozen were wounded. In addition, the Nazis were able to determine how the prisoners had obtained the explosives. Four young women who worked at the factory, including Róza Robota, were arrested by the Gestapo and tortured for several weeks. They were hanged in front of the assembled prisoners on January 6, 1945, just three weeks before the Russian army reached Auschwitz.

The end of Auschwitz

For months, the prisoners of Auschwitz could hear the thunder of cannon fire as the Soviet army moved ever closer. In August 1944, there were approximately 105,000 prisoners in Auschwitz. Beginning around that time, thousands of prisoners were sent by train to concentration camps in Germany.

On November 25, 1944, the order came from Berlin: Himmler wanted the gas chambers and crematoria destroyed. Prisoners, mostly women, began the work of erasing the terrible evidence of the Holocaust. The burned wreck of Crematorium IV, which the *Sonderkommando* had destroyed in their revolt, was demolished. In the other crematoria, the furnaces were taken apart, then the chimneys and the roofs. The piping and ventilation were removed from the gas chambers.

The Nazis also tried to burn all the documents that showed what had happened at Auschwitz. They were afraid that the evidence of their crimes would be captured by the

Russians, which is what had happened at the Majdanek death camp in July 1944.

On January 18, 1945, the evacuation of the camp began. There were still about 65,000 prisoners there, including some 16,000 women. About 58,000 of them were lined up and went through their last roll call at Auschwitz. Then, they marched out with most of the SS men guarding them.

About 6,000 prisoners were left behind because they were too weak to walk. There had been a plan to kill all remaining prisoners before the evacuation, but this would take a long time without the gas chambers. The SS personnel were more interested in escaping from the Soviets than in killing half-dead inmates.

The shells of Crematoria II and III were blown up with dynamite on January 20, 1945; Crematorium V was destroyed some time later. On January 24, the last SS men left. Three days later, the first Russian soldiers reached the camp.

Prisoners of Auschwitz greet their Russian liberators in January 1945.

Primo Levi

Primo Levi was one of those prisoners still in Auschwitz when the first Russian soldiers arrived. Levi was an Italian Jew, a chemist, who spent his entire postwar life writing about the Holocaust. Upon the freeing of the camp by the Russians, he noted that the Russian soldiers "did not greet us, nor did they smile." They did not talk but kept looking at the terrible scene because, according to Levi, they were ashamed. It was the shame that the prisoners had felt after each "selection" and each time they had to witness some outrage at the hands of the Nazis. It was the shame "that the just man experiences at another man's crime; the feeling of guilt that such a crime should exist."

The Auschwitz death march

The temperature was below zero and the cold winter wind was blowing heavily when the Auschwitz prisoners began their march. Few had overcoats. They were divided into different columns, with several thousand prisoners under SS guard in each. The guards pushed them to hurry, sometimes in complete darkness. Prisoners who fell down from exhaustion were shot. As each column of prisoners went by, they could see the bloody bodies from the earlier column lying in the ditch alongside the road. A prisoner in a later column saw a body every 40 or 50 yards for many miles.

The columns were supposed to be headed for the Gross-Rosen concentration camp. Rudolph Höss, the former Auschwitz commander who at this time was supervising concentration camps from his office in Berlin, saw the death march from his car. He wrote in his memoir: "I now met columns of prisoners, struggling through the deep snow. They had no food. Most of the noncommissioned officers in charge of these stumbling columns of corpses had no idea where they were supposed to be going. They only knew that their final destination was Gross-Rosen. But how to get there was a mystery."

Some of the prisoners were able to use the confusion to escape. Twenty-one year old Sara Erenhalt and a group of other women had marched for 24 hours through the snow with no shoes and no food. The SS guards stopped the column in a village and told the prisoners to find a place to sleep. There was no place to lock up the prisoners, and the SS men were probably too tired themselves to guard them all night.

Erenhalt and six others went into a house and asked the old man there if they could sleep in his barn. He turned out to be a priest, and he agreed to hide them, even though SS men were using his house for the night. In the morning, the seven women stayed in the barn instead of rejoining the column. They hid in the priest's barn for three and a half weeks, until Russian soldiers reached the village.

Most of the SS guards were more careful, though. Each column struggled forward, on different routes, through the cold, with little food. They rarely slept. One group reached a

A column of prisoners on a death march from the Dachau concentration camp in April 1945. As they struggled on, prisoners who fell down from exhaustion were shot.

Captured SS troops are forced to load trucks with the dead from Bergen-Belsen concentration camp, 1945.

railroad line after a week. The prisoners were loaded onto open freight cars, with the SS shooting to make them keep their heads down. They lay in the cars for five days, many of them freezing to death, before reaching the Mauthausen concentration camp in Austria, not far from Hilter's hometown. Eight thousand of the Auschwitz prisoners reached the camp alive.

Ten thousand others, including many women, eventually reached the Bergen-Belsen camp in northwestern Germany. Bergen-Belsen had been receiving similar transports of prisoners from the east for some time. It was completely overcrowded and lacking in food, even by concentration camp standards. Epidemics swept through the camp, killing thousands. The British troops who freed the camp in April 1945 found 10,000 bodies lying on the ground. For five days before the British arrived, the people had been without food or water. Fourteen thousand prisoners were so sick or weak that they died even after the camp was freed.

U.S Army generals Dwight Eisenhower, Omar Bradley, and George Patton examine the corpses of prisoners found at the Buchenwald concentration camp in April 1945.

Nearly 60,000 prisoners had been marched out of Auschwitz on January 18, 1945. More than 15,000 died on the march. Many of the others died in places like Mauthausen and Bergen-Belsen.

Other death marches

The Auschwitz death march was the largest of many. During the winter of 1944-45, as Russian troops closed in from the east, the SS drove the prisoners westward to the concentration camps in Germany. In the spring of 1945, during the last months of World War II, the American and British armies approached these camps from the west. The Nazis waited until the last minute to try to evacuate these final camps. Many of the prisoners—some of them the same people who had recently arrived from the east—were marched out again. At this point, though, there was no place left for the SS to go. Between 15,000 and 20,000 prisoners from Dachau, the first concentration camp, were marched aimlessly around the countryside by the SS in groups of different sizes. Many died before the American army reached them.

There is no way to know how many people died during the dozens of death marches staged by the Nazis. Historian Martin Gilbert estimates that several hundred thousand people perished during the marches themselves.

The numbers at Auschwitz

Researchers are still unsure how many people were sent to Auschwitz and how many people died there. Hundreds of thousands of people were sent directly from the transport trains to be killed in the gas chambers. These people were never registered as "official" prisoners of Auschwitz. At first, the Nazis kept very detailed records of the registered prisoners, but as enemy armies approached, they did everything possible to destroy these records.

The first attempt to estimate the number of victims of the camp was commissioned by the Soviet (Russian) government. The commission based its figures on the testimony of eyewitnesses and the capacity of the gas chambers and crematoria. It concluded that at least 4 million people had died at Auschwitz. The Polish commission investigating Auschwitz came up with a similar number.

Rudolph Höss, the commandant of Auschwitz for much of its existence, first said that "at least 2.5 million people were put to death, gassed, and subsequently burned there; in addition, 500,000 people died of exhaustion and illness, which gives a total of 3 million victims." Later, Höss said that these numbers were too high and that the real number was 1.13 million people. In the years since, historians of the Holocaust have estimated many different figures.

Some skeptics use the huge variations in mortality numbers to argue that the Holocaust never happened at all—or that the total number of victims has been *greatly* exaggerated. But even if "only" one million Jews died at Auschwitz itself, the reality of the camp would stay the same. The testimony of many survivors, of Höss and many other Nazis, and the records that have been found all indicate that the Holocaust was very real indeed. (Denial of the Holocaust is discussed in Chapter 14.)

Decades after the Holocaust took place, scholars have tried once again to determine a more accurate number of Auschwitz victims. Although they all agree that the exact number will never be known, they have found ways to try to make their estimates as reliable as possible. Historians have examined the records of the transports that brought people to Auschwitz, the numbers who were deported from the different countries of Europe, and the numbers who survived. Franciszek Piper, the chief historian of the official Auschwitz museum, conducted one of the most careful studies. He believes that at least 1,100,000 people died at Auschwitz, about 1,000,000 of them Jews. The highest estimate that he considers possible is 1,500,000, including 1,350,000 Jews. In addition, many more thousands of people who were transferred from Auschwitz when the camp was evacuated died in the "death marches" or after resettlement in other concentration camps.

10

Life and Death in Nazi-Dominated Europe: Denmark and the Netherlands

The Jews in every country that Germany conquered during World War II (1939–45) were sitting ducks—targets that the Nazis aimed to eliminate in their quest to "cleanse" Europe's population. This chapter describes what happened to the Jews in two German-occupied countries—Denmark and the Netherlands—while Chapter 11 describes their treatment in German-occupied France, and Chapter 12 in the countries of Germany's allies, Italy and Hungary. (A military occupation is said to occur when a victorious country stations military forces on the territory of a defeated country and takes control of the defeated country.)

Differing situations

In each European country occupied by Germany, the Nazis had to implement different strategies to launch the Final Solution—the

Nazi term for the organized murder of the Jewish people. The Jewish population of some of these countries, mainly those in eastern Europe, were isolated from the non-Jewish majority. Especially in the small towns, the lives of the Jews were centered on their synagogues (houses of worship) and the study of the Jewish religion. Many eastern European Jews dressed differently, had different jobs, and spoke a different language (Yiddish) than the other people in the area.

In western Europe, on the other hand, most Jews lived side by side with non-Jews, read the same books, and saw the same movies. This generation of Jews consisted mainly of people who were less staunch in their religious ideals than their grandparents, and they married non-Jews much more often than did the Jews of eastern Europe. (Jews who blended into the larger society in this way were said to be assimilated.)

In some European countries such as Poland, the Jews constituted a large minority. In others—Italy and Denmark among them—Jews made up only a tiny proportion of the population. While it is true that the Jews of Europe faced widespread antisemitism (anti-Jewish sentiment), the intensity of the prejudice varied from country to country.

Although the people of all the countries conquered by Germany suffered terribly, some were treated much more brutally than others, especially at the beginning of the war. In these hard-hit countries, the process of murdering the Jews began earlier and netted far more victims.

The Nazi Party's deeply entrenched sense of racism affected how the Nazis treated both the non-Jewish and the Jewish population of conquered territory. For example, the Nazis believed that many eastern Europeans—like the Russians—were greatly inferior to Germans. The mass murder of the Jews of these Soviet areas began immediately, even though it often caused economic problems for the Germans. On the other hand, the German army played a much less direct part in deporting Jews from western Europe, where they treated the local population less harshly, at least at first. For example, many historians believe that Denmark received special treatment from the Germans when it was first conquered because the Nazis thought of the Danes as "racial cousins."

A group portrait of a Jewish resistance group in Poland in 1940.

Differences among the Nazis

The SS (the abbreviation used for the *Schutzstaffel*), the Nazi organization in charge of executing the plans for the destruction of the Jews, wanted to carry out Nazi racial goals in every country under German occupation as soon as possible. But despite the growing power of the SS in the German government, obstacles to their goals arose within their own government. The German army did not want to have to fight against resistance groups throughout Europe, so for them it was not practical to create a furor among the people of the conquered country. German officials were also afraid of disrupting the economy of the occupied countries. They wanted to use the resources of the country for the benefit of Germany and the German war effort. The German officials who quarreled with the SS over their plans to destroy the Jewish population were not trying to protect the Jews—they simply had other priorities. But the bickering between government agencies usually led to a slowdown in the Nazis' actions against the Jews of the affected region.

National governments under German occupation

The amount of power the SS held in a particular country was closely related to the strength of that country's government. In Poland and the conquered parts of the Soviet Union (Russia), the Nazis completely abolished the existing governments and took direct control of all subsequent administrative activity. Here the SS was at its strongest. In other occupied countries such as Denmark and France, however, the Germans allowed a national government to remain in existence. Still others fell between the two extremes, with Germans officially eliminating the national government but allowing the day-to-day administration of the country to be carried out by citizens of the conquered country. The Germans had neither the time nor the manpower to run the local police, the courts, the railroads, or the many other operations of each country they conquered. This gave the governments and administrators of occupied countries some bargaining power. Likewise, Germany's allies—countries like Italy and Hungary that sided with Germany in the war—were given considerable leeway in their political and economic affairs. The Nazis needed the cooperation of the Italian and Hungarian governments to keep their forces fighting alongside the German army.

The Germans wanted the conquered countries of Europe to help in the killing of the Jews. It would have been difficult, for example, for the Germans to station enough of their own police forces to control a large country like France, so the Nazis sought the cooperation of the French police in rounding up Jews. In this way, the lives of the Jews themselves became "bargaining chips." The government of an occupied country might agree to let the Nazis deport that country's Jews, or some of them, in return for a deal on other issues. On the other hand, a government that was determined to protect the Jews could refuse to cooperate in arresting them. Such actions were chancy, though, since the occupied country risked retaliatory action (revenge for noncooperation) from the Nazis.

Bargaining with the Nazis

The bargaining and negotiations between the Germans and the countries they controlled changed as the war continued. At first, it looked like Germany would win the war and the Nazis would control Europe for the foreseeable future. At that time the ability of German allies and of German-occupied countries to resist German demands was very limited, because Germany's military power was great enough to force them to do what Germany wanted. If they thought it was necessary, the Nazis would simply wipe out the occupied country's government and impose direct military rule over the land.

When the armies of the Allies (the Soviet Union, Great Britain, and the United States) began to push the Germans back, and Germany's prospect of winning the war decreased, the bargaining power of the occupied countries increased. At the same time, however, the Nazis became more determined to wipe out all the Jews—even if Germany lost the war. In the last years of the war, the survival of the Jews became a question of time—every delay in the Nazi plan meant that more Jews would be alive when Germany was finally defeated. Still, hundreds of thousands of Jews died because the Nazis succeeded in deporting them only a few weeks—or even days—before the Allied troops could reach them.

In other words, the lives of millions of human beings depended on many different factors that were beyond their control. The Jews were more likely to survive in a country that maintained some independence from the Germans—and especially from the SS. Similarly, the Jews had a greater chance for survival in a country whose government and people did not share the Nazis' intense antisemitism. Even geography played an important part in the Jewish struggle; some Jews found safety by escaping to nearby countries not involved in the war; others survived because the Allied armies arrived on the scene before the Nazis could kill them.

Denmark

Denmark is a small country. It had a population of only 4 million in 1940, when Germany invaded it. (At that time, the population of the United States was about 130 million, while Germany had 65 million people.) More than half the people of Denmark lived in the capital city of Copenhagen.

The rest lived mostly in small towns and on farms (largely dairy farms). There were also many fisherman among its people. Much of Denmark is made up of islands. At its closest point, the nation is situated less than three miles across a strait from its neighbor, Sweden.

There were about 6,500 Danish Jews in 1940. Like other Jews in western Europe, they were much more assimilated than the Jews of eastern Europe. Many Danish Jews were professionals—doctors, lawyers, scientists. Others had government jobs or were involved in banking. In addition, Danish Jews had one of the highest rates of marriage with non-Jews in the world.

Also, there were about 1,500 Jewish refugees in Denmark who had come from Germany, Austria, and Czechoslovakia, which had recently been taken over by Germany. (Refugees are people who flee to a foreign country to escape danger or persecution.) Many thousands of Jews from all over Europe had passed through Denmark on their way to other countries since 1933, when the escape from the Nazis was in its infancy. The Danish government was willing to accept them temporarily, but—like most countries—opposed the idea of allowing large numbers of Jewish refugees to settle within its borders.

Mild treatment

When Germany invaded Denmark in April 1940, the small Danish army, faced with hopeless odds, offered almost no resistance. The German occupation of Denmark began relatively peacefully, and the Germans seemed to want to maintain a noncombative atmosphere. They allowed the Danish government to remain in office and to continue administering the country. The regular Danish police carried on its normal functions, and the Germans even allowed the Danish army and navy to continue in existence. The agreement between Germany and Denmark also included a statement that Germany would not mistreat the Danish Jews. Of course, the presence of German troops occupying the country meant that Germany would have the final say on any issue important to it. Some historians feel that the Nazis' relatively mild treatment of Denmark may have resulted from the party's racial philosophy. Germans tended to view the Danes as relatives, fellow members of the Aryan race. (See box on p. 6.)

Denmark was also the first country in western Europe conquered by Germany. Experts speculate that the Germans wanted to use Denmark as a model—a way to show other countries that being defeated by Germany was not as catastrophic as first thought. In addition, the lack of military resistance by the Danish armed forces and the comparatively few acts of sabotage (destruction of military or industrial equipment) against the Germans at the beginning of the occupation probably influenced German policy in Denmark's favor. A peaceful and cooperative Denmark meant large shipments of butter and meat could be sent to help feed Germany. Besides, Germany did not want to tie down combat troops in Denmark because they faced much larger battles elsewhere. In neighboring Norway, for instance, the German occupation was met with fierce and violent resistance from the beginning.

Many of the German soldiers stationed in Denmark after the invasion were older men in their forties and even fifties. Most of them had grown up—and developed their own personal beliefs and philosophies—before the Nazis came to power. Few were enthusiastic Nazis. Many of these troops, including the officers, were reluctant to get involved in attacking or arresting Jews.

Danish attitudes

While the Danes offered almost no military resistance to the Germans at the beginning of the occupation, they did resist Nazi ideas and propaganda. (Propaganda is distorted information to promote ideas or a program.) The Danish government agreed to most German demands, even restrictions on the traditional Danish freedom of the press. But it refused to pass anti-Jewish laws or to fire Jews from government jobs. Jewish students were not expelled from schools or universities. Religious services continued to be held. Danish law made it a crime to incite (provoke) antisemitic acts, and this law remained on the books even though it could not be enforced.

The tiny minority of Danish Nazis were treated with contempt by most of the nation's people. The Danish Nazi newspaper *The Fatherland* was called "The Traitorland" by the anti-Nazi Danes.

The Danes' view of the Jews has been immortalized in a legend that grew out of the war era. According to the story, the Germans planned to order all Danish Jews to wear the six-pointed Jewish star as a form of identification—an order they had enforced in the other countries they occupied. Learning of the plan, King Christian X is said to have put a Jewish star on his uniform, wearing it on his daily horseback ride through the streets of Copenhagen. The message of this story is clear: the Jews were part of the Danish nation, fellow countrymen who were not to be treated differently than non-Jewish Danes.

The German plan

In late 1942, German policy toward Denmark changed drastically. Denmark was slated to become part of Germany. Top German officials in Denmark were replaced by tougher, more committed Nazis. The Danes resisted German pressure. Acts of sabotage increased dramatically. A wave of strikes swept the country as workers protested various German regulations. In August 1943, the Germans declared a state of martial law in Denmark and sent their troops into Copenhagen. (Martial law is military law that operates in a country during a state of emergency.) The Danish army was disarmed and the government was dissolved.

The Germans proceeded to arrest and deport the Danish Jews with the personal approval of German leader Adolf Hitler. The mass arrests were planned for the night of October 1, 1943—the second night of Rosh Hashanah, the Jewish New Year (an important religious holiday), when most Jews would be at home.

Rescue

Word of the Nazis' plan for the Jews was leaked to the Danes from sympathetic Germans in the occupation administration. The Danes passed the message to every Jew they could find. One non-Jewish Dane named Jorgen Knudsen, an ambulance driver in Copenhagen, found names in the phone book that he thought sounded Jewish. He visited each of these people in his ambulance to warn them of the Germans' plans. Jews who had nowhere else to go were shuttled to the hospital in his ambulance, where they were temporarily hidden.

Jewish refugees are ferried out of Denmark aboard Danish fishing boats bound for Sweden.

Strangers approached Jews on the street and offered them the keys to their apartments to hide. Thousands of other Danish Jews were hidden by their non-Jewish neighbors and friends and smuggled out of Copenhagen (where most Jews lived) to smaller towns on the coast. All of this was done while the Germans continued to search for the hidden Jews—though many of the German patrols seemed to "look the other way." The Danish police refused to cooperate with the Germans in the search. In fact, they helped escort the Jews to the coast.

From there, Danish fishing boats ferried the Jews across the strait to Sweden, which was not occupied by Germany. The Swedish government announced that it would accept all Danish Jews. The small boats, crowded with refugees, sailed from various Danish towns, avoiding the patrols of the German navy.

The evacuation of the Jews from Copenhagen took three weeks. During this time, the university closed for a week so that the students could help in the operation. Many Danish organizations publicly protested the German action. On Sunday, October 3, 1943, Danish ministers read a letter of protest in their churches. The letter stated that the persecution of the Jews was un-Christian and that the Danish church would obey the laws of God—not the laws of Germans. A large proportion of the Danish people were actively involved in saving the Jews. Practically all Danes knew what was happening; none are known to have helped the Germans.

An unanswered question

About 7,200 Jews, along with 700 of their non-Jewish relatives, were transported safely to Sweden. The Germans succeeded in arresting between 400 and 500 Danish and foreign Jews. The Danish government protested these arrests and demanded assurances from the Germans that the arrestees would be treated properly. The Jews from Denmark were sent to the concentration camp at Theresienstadt, in what had been Czechoslovakia. (Concentration camps were prisons where the Nazis confined "enemies of the state." See box on Theresienstadt on p. 294.) A delegation of the Danish government was eventually allowed to inspect the camp's conditions.

The property of the Danish Jews—those who had escaped to Sweden and those arrested by the Germans—was carefully preserved. No one took over their homes or stole their furniture. The Danes removed the sacred Torah scrolls (the first five books of the Bible) from Jewish synagogues for safekeeping. They sent food packages to the deported Jews. Unlike so many others from Theresienstadt, the Danish Jews as a group were never sent to Auschwitz to be killed. Fifty-four died at Theresienstadt; one died at Auschwitz.

Of the 8,000 Jews in Denmark on the day of the German invasion, less than 100 died at the hands of the Nazis: 55 did not survive deportation, about 20 died during the escape to Sweden, and about 20 others committed suicide rather than be captured by the Germans. No other country controlled by Germany saved so high a proportion of its Jewish population.

The conditions of Denmark were unusual, and perhaps no other country could have done the same. But what hap-

Theresienstadt

Theresienstadt (Terezin in the Czech language) was the only concentration camp the Nazis ever allowed outsiders to inspect. They set up a "model ghetto" there that differed significantly from the reality of other concentration camps. The inmates of this "model ghetto" supposedly ran their own affairs as a self-governing Jewish community. Among the prisoners were well-known German Jews—artists, writers, and scientists whose disappearance would have raised too many questions in foreign countries. Together, the inmates organized several orchestras, a choir, and a library with 60,000 books. They also held Jewish religious services on a regular basis.

The Nazis used Theresienstadt to try to convince the Danes, as well as the rest of the world, that conditions in the camps were humane. Representatives of the International Red Cross were allowed to visit the camp. Just before the visit, however, the Nazis spruced up the place considerably, opening a school and kindergartens, a coffeehouse and other stores, and a bank. They even planted flowers. They also reduced the overcrowding in the camp, but did so at a high cost to the Jews—they sent some of the camp's inmates to Auschwitz to be killed.

So the "reality" that the Red Cross representatives saw was a terrible deception. Apart from the well-known few, Theresienstadt's inmates were usually there only temporarily. Most were quickly sent off to Auschwitz, where they were murdered. The fact that the Jews arrested in Denmark remained in Theresienstadt shows that the pressure of the Danish government, and of Danish public opinion, may have had some effect on Nazi policy. Unlike the overwhelming majority of Jews who were sent to Theresienstadt, more than 85 percent of the Danish Jews survived.

pened in Denmark leads to one of the great unanswered questions of the Holocaust: what would have happened if the ordinary people of other nations—of France, of Lithuania, or of Germany itself—had acted like the Danes?

The Netherlands

The Netherlands was one of the countries whose people tried hardest to save the Jews, but it was also one of the countries in which the fewest Jews survived. The course of the Holocaust took a terrible turn in this country during the early 1940s.

The Netherlands is a western European country located to the northwest of Germany. The name means "lowlands"—much of the country is below sea level. A network of dikes

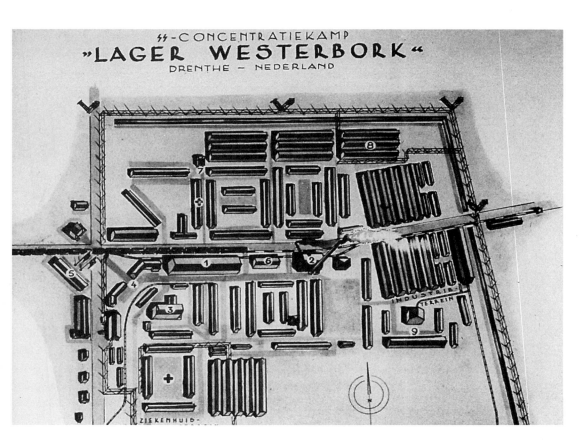

SS-CONCENTRATIEKAMP
"LAGER WESTERBORK"
DRENTHE — NEDERLAND

crisscrosses the land, holding back the waters of the North Sea. In English, the Netherlands is often called "Holland" (although Holland makes up only one section of the country), and its people and language are termed "Dutch." The Dutch language is a close relative of German, but the Netherlands has a history that differs significantly from that of Germany. When World War II began, the Netherlands was neutral—allied neither with Great Britain and France nor with Germany. It wanted to stay out of the war, just as it had stayed out of World War I (1914–18). But as a democratic country, the Netherlands sympathized with Britain and France and opposed the Nazi dictatorship in Germany.

Under the influence of Germany, a small Dutch Nazi Party existed, but it did not have great support. The antisemitism of the Dutch Nazis was something new in the Netherlands, and most Dutch people rejected it. Jews had lived in the Netherlands for hundreds of years. Some had come from Spain and Portugal in the sixteenth and seven-

A map of the Westerbork camp. Until July 1942, Westerbork was a refugee camp for Jews who had moved illegally to the Netherlands.

teenth centuries. Most of the Dutch thought of the Jews of their country as fellow citizens, not as outsiders.

The antisemitic laws passed in Germany and the terrible treatment of German Jews in the years under Hitler shocked most of the Dutch. About 30,000 Jewish refugees, mostly from Germany, went to the Netherlands to escape the Nazis. By 1940, there were about 140,000 Jews in the Netherlands—about 1.6 percent of the population of almost 9,000,000. About 75,000 Jews, more than half, lived in Amsterdam, the largest city. Amsterdam had a larger proportion of Jews than any other big city in western Europe.

Most Dutch Jews outside of Amsterdam were relatively well-off, working in business and in professions like law, medicine, and education. This was also true for many who lived in Amsterdam, where Jews played an important role in the diamond trade (buying and selling, cutting and polishing the precious stones—Amsterdam was the world center of this industry). There were, however, about 40,000 impoverished Amsterdam Jews who lived in the old Jewish neighborhood and other areas near the harbor. Many of the men worked as sailors, longshoremen (people who load and unload ships), and other dockworkers in the port.

Invasion and occupation

Although the Netherlands was politically neutral, Nazi Germany still considered it a prime target. In April 1940, Germany had invaded Denmark and Norway, which were also neutral. Then, on the night of May 9, the German air force, the *Luftwaffe,* bombed military targets throughout the Netherlands without any warning. German paratroopers seized the bridges near the port of Rotterdam, and German tanks and infantry rolled over the border. The Dutch army resisted but the Germans threatened to bomb Dutch cities. Queen Wilhelmina and the Dutch government escaped to England, and the Netherlands surrendered on May 14. While the terms of the surrender were being negotiated, the *Luftwaffe* bombed Rotterdam, completely destroying the center of the city.

This was a sign of things to come. The German occupation of the Netherlands was the harshest of any country in western Europe. The relative percentage of Jews who died at

the hands of the Nazis was much higher in the Netherlands than in neighboring Belgium or France. Only in eastern Europe and in the areas that became part of Germany itself did the Nazis succeed in killing a higher ratio of Jews than in the Netherlands.

Some historians believe the reason for this stemmed from the basic German theory of race. The Nazis apparently thought of the Dutch as members of a German "tribe" that had been separated from Germany. (See box on p. 25.)The party's main goal in occupying the Netherlands was to "reclaim" the region as quickly as possible. The immediate elimination of the Jews from the country was a prerequisite to Germany's recovery of this supposedly "lost" territory.

Attack and resistance

The Nazis appointed Artur Seyss-Inquart to run the Netherlands with absolute power. Seyss-Inquart was an Austrian Nazi who had played an important part in Germany's

A photo of the center of Rotterdam destroyed by German bombing in May 1940. The bombing of Rotterdam was a sign of things to come.

takeover of Austria in 1938. (See Chapter 4, p. 106.) For a few months, he served as one of the top German officials in Poland, where the Nazi plans to destroy the Jews were already far advanced. (See Chapters 5 and 6.) Seyss-Inquart immediately announced the exclusion of Jews from the terms of the Netherlands' surrender, terms that guaranteed certain civil rights to the Dutch people under German occupation. The Jews, he said, were an enemy with whom it was impossible to make peace.

Soon a series of official orders were leveled against the Dutch Jews. Jewish-owned businesses were taken over. All Jewish government employees were "suspended" from their jobs. Jewish professors were dismissed from universities. This led to protests by Dutch students and to student strikes at the universities of Delft and Leiden, which the Germans then closed. In January 1941, all Dutch citizens with at least one Jewish grandparent had to register with the authorities.

In February 1941, a crowd of Dutch Nazis marched into the Jewish section of Amsterdam and began to smash windows, set fire to synagogues, and beat up Jews. Just as they did in eastern Europe, the Germans wanted it to appear as if the local population hated Jews as much as the Nazis did. They secretly helped organize anti-Jewish riots that were supposed to be the "spontaneous" actions of the people of the Netherlands, not the Germans. But this plan did not work in Amsterdam. The people of the Jewish neighborhood, including non-Jews, began fighting back. They succeeded in driving the Dutch Nazis out of the area. The Nazis returned later the same day, only to face a well-prepared force of Jews, including many longshoremen and factory workers. Patrols armed with lead pipes guarded Jewish shops, and the Dutch Nazis were beaten back in a series of street battles. Many non-Jewish Dutch citizens also took part in these actions.

Three battalions of German police—armed with automatic weapons and tanks—were sent in to "restore order" to Amsterdam. Many Jews were injured, and the Germans sealed off the neighborhood by raising the bridges surrounding it. At this point, the Germans ordered the creation of a single Jewish Council (*Joodse Raad* in Dutch) made up of prominent Jews. The council's job was to transmit German orders to the Jewish community. This was somewhat similar to the administrative structure in Poland, where the Nazis had established a Jewish Council, called a *Judenrat,* in each community. (See Chapter 5, pp. 126–27.)

The February strike

A few days later, another violent incident took place: German police were attacked with acid as they entered a Jewish shop in Amsterdam. In revenge, the Germans arrested over 400 Jews off the streets of Amsterdam and sent them to a concentration camp in Germany. Only one of them survived the war.

Led by the longshoremen, both Jewish and non-Jewish Dutch workers, went on strike to protest this action. Public services, transportation, and large factories stopped operations. The city of Amsterdam was virtually shut down for three days. The strike spread to two nearby cities, leaving the Germans dangerously close to losing control of the country. They declared a state of martial law and sent large numbers of troops into the city to force people back to work. Strikers faced arrest and deportation to a German concentration camp—or even the prospect of being shot on the spot. A heavy "fine" was imposed on the country in punishment for the strike. In the end, the Germans succeeded in ending the protests.

One of the factors that helped end the strike was that the *Joodse Raad* urged the people of Amsterdam to go back to work. The SS, the Nazi organization charged with carryng out the elimnation of the Jews, threatened severe action against the Jews of the Netherlands if the strike continued. The *Joodse Raad* wanted to prevent harm to Jews and to all the Dutch, and they thought that obeying the Nazis would ensure the population's safety. No one knew that the Nazis would try to kill all the Jews anyway.

Setting the Jews apart

Leading Dutch Jews who opposed the *Joodse Raad*'s policy joined together to form the Jewish Coordinating Council. Its leader was Lodewijk Visser, who had been the presiding judge on the Dutch Supreme Court until he was removed by the Nazis. Visser did not want the Jewish community of the Netherlands to deal directly with the Nazis. Instead, he wanted the Nazis to transmit their orders

A deportation point in Amsterdam, the Netherlands. By October 1942, British radio reported that Jews deported from Western Europe were being gassed.

through the regular Dutch authorities, as they did for everyone else. To Visser and his supporters, the formation of a *Joodse Raad* was dangerous because it separated the country's Jews from its non-Jews.

Everywhere in German-occupied Europe, the Nazis tried to isolate the Jews from the rest of the conquered peoples. The desire to segregate—or "mark"—the Jews led to the mandate, or order, that all Jews wear a Jewish star on their clothing at all times. This requirement took effect in the Netherlands beginning in May 1942. Earlier, in the summer of 1941, other antisemitic laws had come into force in the Netherlands. Jews were forbidden from entering museums or movie theaters, or even walking on certain streets. They were not allowed outside at night. They could shop only at certain times of the day. Additional Nazi laws restricted where Jews could live and prevented them from working side by side with non-Jews. Even Jewish children were segregated—they were not allowed to attend the same schools as their non-Jewish friends and neighbors. Jewish students were expelled from Dutch preparatory schools in August 1941 and from the universities in 1942.

All Jews who were Dutch citizens were ordered to move to Amsterdam by January 1942. Those who were not citizens were supposed to be sent to a camp at Westerbork in the eastern part of the country. Westerbork became a transit camp from which the Jews of the Netherlands were sent to the death camps of eastern Europe.

The Nazis wanted the majority of people—the non-Jews—in German-occupied countries to feel that anti-Jewish actions had nothing to do with them, that this was strictly a "Jewish problem." Convincing non-Jewish Europeans that Jews weren't really part of their nation was a Nazi strategy to create a sense of indifference—a disconnectedness—among the non-Jewish peoples of Europe that would leave them less committed to guarding Jewish interests.

A lost opportunity?

The February 1941 strike in Amsterdam was a way of rejecting the Nazis' strategy. By striking to protest the harsh treatment of Jews, the Dutch were saying that attacking the Jews was attacking all Dutch people. The Dutch workers had many other reasons to hate the Nazis, and the strike was not held solely in protest of anti-Jewish actions. But the strike did ignite a feeling of rebellion that led to more and more protests against the arrest and deportation of Jews.

No one can say what would have happened if the *Joodse Raad* had urged the strikers to continue their protest. Two schools of thought have arisen on the subject. According to some experts, a continuation of the strike would no doubt have resulted in a bloodbath. Soldiers probably would have shot hundreds of strikers, and the Dutch Jews would almost certainly have been hunted down and murdered even sooner. In addition, the members of the Jewish Council themselves would have been in serious danger.

Opposing historians believe that the fear of constant trouble from the Dutch might have caused the Nazis to slow down their anti-Jewish actions. Perhaps all the laws and orders against the Jews that came into effect during 1941 and 1942 would have taken longer to enforce. That could have meant a delay in the later parts of the Nazi plan—the arrests, deportations, and deaths. And delay might have meant that more Jews would have survived until Germany was defeated in the war.

Continued resistance and deadly rumors

The February strike was the largest single protest by occupied-Europe's non-Jews against the Nazis' anti-Jewish actions. There were no more mass protests of this kind in the Netherlands after the defeat of the strike. But the Dutch consistently expressed opposition to Nazi ideas about Jews and they continued to resist separating the Jews from the rest of the Dutch population. When the Nazis ordered all Jews to wear a yellow six-pointed Jewish star, many non-Jewish Dutch people also put the stars on their clothing. (In neighboring Belgium, thousands of non-Jews wore Jewish stars, sometimes in the colors of the Belgian flag.) Many other Dutch people wore a yellow flower on their clothes to show their support of the Jews. Illegal posters urged people to tip their hats in a show of respect when they passed Jews on the street.

The Protestant and Catholic Churches urged Christians to refuse to cooperate with anti-Jewish orders. One letter read in many churches said that "no compromise in this domain of conscience [could be] allowed." The letter told the Dutch that refusing to cooperate was necessary to fulfill "your duty to God and man" even if it led to personal sacrifices—in other words, even if it put someone's life in danger. In fact, about 20,000 non-Jewish Dutch people were sent to concentration camps for opposing the Nazis' antisemitism.

Then the Dutch began to learn about the death camps. Many able-bodied Jewish men, like many non-Jews, had already been sent to labor camps in the Dutch countryside to work for the Germans. At first, the Jews were treated just like everyone else in the camps. Then, in June 1942, the Germans announced that all Jews would be sent to labor camps in Germany. Because the German order included even children, people became suspicious: why would small children be sent to a labor camp? Soon there were rumors that the Jews were being sent to their deaths. By October 1942, the Dutch were hearing reports on the British radio that Jews deported from western Europe were being gassed.

Inmates at forced labor hauling cartloads of earth at the Mauthausen concentration camp, where many Dutch opponents of the Nazis were sent.

Deportations and rescues

The Germans began a series of raids to round up Jews, but the Dutch police would not cooperate. In the fall of 1942, German soldiers and Nazi Party members—in addition to the police—were given the power to arrest Jews. Jews were seized in their homes late at night and taken to the camp at Westerbork. From there, sealed in cattle cars, they were sent by train to Poland to be killed. On October 2, all the Jews in the Dutch labor camps were captured and sent to Westerbork.

An arriving transport of Dutch Jews at Westerbork. In July 1942, Westerbork became a transit camp from which the Jews of the Netherlands were sent to the death camps of eastern Europe.

As soon as the arrests began, thousands of non-Jewish Dutch people tried to hide the Jews who refused to report for deportation. This was not easy in the Netherlands. The country is heavily populated, with few remote areas where people might be hidden without attracting attention. There are no mountains or large forests. Most Dutch houses do not even have cellars because of the danger of flooding. In addition, the Netherlands did not border on any neutral country like Switzerland or Sweden where Jews might be smuggled. Ferrying Jews to safety meant a long and dangerous trip through Belgium and France, which were also occupied by Germany. Successful escapes called for crossing borders that were guarded by German patrols. This was accomplished either by sneaking across the borders or by showing false identity papers to officials stationed there. False papers were needed to ride on a train, and escaping Jews needed provisions—food and a safe place to sleep—during the trip.

A Survivor Remembers

"Cross this difficult road successfully and build your homeland, a homeland for the whole Jewish people. But do not forget that you are bound to all humanity, something which you perhaps learned in Holland. Do not forget us, your non-Jewish comrades."

—Joop Westerweel's farewell words to a group of Jews he had led to the Spanish border.

Joachim Simon, known as "Shushu," together with his wife, Adina, organized one of the best-known escape routes for Dutch Jews. Simon was a German Jew in his early twenties who had traveled to the Netherlands as a refugee in 1938. As the Germans began rounding up Dutch Jews, he managed to obtain false papers and gain entry into France. He then set up a series of contacts all the way to the Pyrenees Mountains on the border between France and neutral Spain. Next, Simon returned to the Netherlands, then led three separate groups of Dutch Jews to safety in Spain. As he was returning from his third successful mission, Simon was arrested crossing the Belgian-Dutch border. He was tortured by the *Geheime Staatspolizei,* or the Gestapo, the secret police, in an effort to make him reveal the names of the people who had helped him. Eventually, afraid that he would not be strong enough to remain silent throughout the torment, Simon took his own life by slashing his wrists.

One of the Dutch people who worked with Simon was Joop Westerweel, a high school principal in the town of Lundsrecht. Westerweel, who had four children, was not Jewish. In February 1943, he personally led a group through France to the Pyrenees. Like Simon, he returned to the Netherlands to continue his rescue missions. For more than a year, he hid Jews and ran a network that got them to Spain or Switzerland. In March 1944, Westerweel was captured and sent to a concentration camp. He was tortured for five months and finally executed.

A Jewish child (far right) poses with the Dutch family that adopted her.

Hiding and capture

The long trip to Spain or Switzerland was extremely difficult to organize and carry out. Trips occurred infrequently and could only accommodate small numbers of people. Because there was no real chance for most of them to escape, the majority of the Jews of the Netherlands had to hide until the war was over. For this, they needed the help of many non-Jews—to provide a hiding place in their homes, to bring them food (which was becoming more and more scarce), and to protect them when the Germans asked questions.

Thousands of Dutch people came to the aid of the Jews. An estimated 25,000 Jews were hidden in the Netherlands, including around 4,000 children. Almost a third of the total number of Jews, somewhere between 7,000 and 8,000, were eventually caught by the Nazis. Even if many people worked hard to hide Jews, all it took was one informer to tell the Nazis. Despite the odds, though, 16,000 people were saved.

The story of the Jews hidden in the Netherlands became famous after the war. One of the families who settled in Amsterdam were the Franks, German Jews who had fled to the city in 1934 to escape Hitler's anti-Jewish policies. They had a young daughter named Anne who lived in Amsterdam from the time she was five years old. In July 1942, when Anne was 13, her 16-year-old sister, Margot, was ordered to report for forced labor in Germany. Fearing that Margot would be sent to her death, the entire Frank family went into hiding. The Franks lived with four other people in rooms hidden in the back of the building where her father's business was located.

Anne Frank

Anne Frank was a very talented writer, and if she had lived she might have become a great one. To escape the Nazis, she hid with her family in secret rooms behind her father's Amsterdam store for more than two years. The family was eventually betrayed. She died at age 15 at the Bergen-Belsen concentration camp. From her diary, we know that Anne was frightened, hopeful, angry, and kind. She seems to have been a very complex person, proud of her Jewish heritage and proud of being Dutch.

Anne began writing in the diary two days after she received it as a present on her thirteenth birthday. Each entry in the diary is addressed to "Kitty."

The following is an excerpt of the diary entry for June 6, 1944. Anne and the others had just heard on their illegal radio that the American and British armies had landed in Normandy, on the coast of France, to begin the liberation of Europe from the Nazis:

Oh, Kitty, the best part of the invasion is that I have the feeling that friends are approaching. We have been oppressed by those terrible Germans for so long, they have had their knives so at our throats, that the thought of friends and delivery fills us with confidence!

Now it doesn't concern the Jews any more; no, it concerns Holland and all occupied Europe. Perhaps, Margot says, I may yet be able to go back to school in September or October.

The family hid there for 25 months, never going out, keeping quiet during the day when people were working in the rest of the building. Non-Jewish employees of her father's business, risking their lives, brought them food, clothing, and books to read. In August 1944, however, the Nazis found the eight hidden Jews. An informer, probably someone who worked in the warehouse, had apparently tipped them off.

The non-Jews who had helped the Franks were arrested and sent to labor camps. The eight hidden Jews were sent first to Westerbork and then to Auschwitz. Most of them were strong enough to work, so they were not murdered immediately. Anne's mother died there from exhaustion and starvation. As the Russian army neared Auschwitz late in 1944, the Nazis moved Anne and Margot from the camp. They were sent to the concentration camp at Bergen-Belsen in Germany. Bergen-Belsen was vastly overcrowded, with little food and no sanitation. Diseases spread quickly among the inmates. Anne's father was left behind at Auschwitz.

During the time she spent hiding in Amsterdam, Anne Frank wrote a diary, documenting her life in what she called the "secret annex." After the war, the diary was published, first in the Netherlands, then in France, then worldwide. Millions of people have read it since then. Anne's story was adapted for the stage and then for film. Anne died of typhus at Bergen-Belsen in late February or early March 1945, soon after her sister, Margot. She was three months short of her sixteenth birthday.

For many people around the world, reading the *Diary of Anne Frank* became a way to learn about the Jewish experience in Europe during the Holocaust. Among all those who died in the Holocaust—old people and babies, strong young men and women in the prime of their lives, teenagers like Anne—her name is probably the best known. She was one of the 107,000 Jews who were deported from the Netherlands by the Nazis out of the 140,000 who had been in the country on the day of the invasion. Sixty thousand, like Anne and her family, were sent to Auschwitz. Thirty-four thousand were sent to the death camp at Sobibór in eastern Poland. (See Chapter 8.) About 5,500 survived deportation, including Anne's father, who was freed when the Russian army reached Auschwitz in January 1945. By the time Otto Frank returned to Amsterdam after the war and found his daughter's diary, three-quarters of the Jews in the Netherlands had died.

11

Life and Death in Nazi-Dominated
Europe: France

During the German occupation, France had a new government that included many anti-Semites, people who were intensely prejudiced against Jews. Many of the officials in the French government went out of their way to cooperate with the Germans. France actually passed vicious anti-Jewish laws. The French authorities made lists of Jews and where they lived, and the French police helped round them up for deportation, or forcibly removing them from the towns in which they lived. The transit camps where they were taken before being deported were guarded by Frenchmen. Despite these factors, three-quarters of the Jews in France survived.

France divided

The German occupation intensified a conflict among the French people that had been growing for over a century. This conflict took many different forms and was in the end really about whether France should become a democracy (a government ruled by the people). At times the main issue was whether France should be a monarchy (ruled by royalty) or a republic (ruled by representatives of the people). At other times the role of the Catholic Church in the nation's educational system was questioned—an issue that centered on the policy of the strict separation of church and state. Other disagreements revolved around the power invested in the French army. Quarreling and deep divisions grew among the French, and somehow the question of Jewish rights became tangled in this web of clashing political opinions. Even though the basic issues of France's political future had nothing to do with the Jews, attitudes toward the Jewish people became a major battleground in the nation's continuing wartime struggle.

Léon Blum, leader of the French Socialist Party, was prime minister of France from 1936 to 1938. He was Jewish. Though France had a history of antismitism, it also had a long history of treating Jews as equals.

Antisemitism grew sharply in France during the 1930s. Groups similar to the Nazis sprang up, although they never became as large and well organized as the German party. More and more European countries were becoming dictatorships, and many of these countries were openly antisemitic. Some French politicians viewed these dictatorships as models that France should follow.

On the other hand, France had a long tradition of treating Jews as equals. It had been the first country in Europe to give the Jewish people full civil rights. (This tradition was one of the reasons that German leader Adolf Hitler hated France so much.) During the worldwide economic depression in the 1930s, France had even had a Jewish prime minister, Léon Blum (pronounced "Bloom"), the leader of the French Socialist Party.

Blum had led a coalition, or union, of parties, including the French Communists, called the "Popular Front" or "People's Front." (Communism is a political and economic theory advocating the formation of a classless society through the communal, or group, ownership of all property.) Much of its

The Dreyfus Affair

Even though foreign-born Jews viewed France as a safe haven from German leader Adolf Hitler and his Nazi Party, France had its own history of antisemitism. In 1894, Captain Alfred Dreyfus, the first Jewish officer to be appointed to the General Staff of the French Army, was falsely accused of treason and sentenced to life in prison. Long buried anti-Jewish sentiments now surfaced, and in some places Jews were attacked on the streets.

Although Dreyfus was eventually found innocent and released from prison, the Dreyfus Affair would have longlasting effects in France. The case prompted Austrian journalist Theodor Herzl to take action. Long a proponent of a Jewish homeland, Herzl believed that the Jews would never be accepted in modern Europe and would always be victims of prejudice. In response to the affair Herzl wrote:

> The Dreyfus case [is] more than a judicial error, it [shows] the desire of ... the French to condemn a Jew, and to condemn all Jews in this one Jew. "Death to the Jews!" howled the mob....

Herzl's words seemed to come true during the Holocaust when the French were willing to hand thousands of Jews over to the Nazis.

support came from French workers. When the Popular Front was elected into office, a wave of factory takeovers and labor strikes swept French industry. The new government sided with the strikers, who organized work stoppages to obtain higher wages and other improvements for workers.

For many French people, the Popular Front represented the promise of a better life for ordinary people. But many others hated everything it stood for. To them, Blum and the Popular Front were the very symbols of what was wrong with France. Opponents of the Popular Front feared the influence of the Communists; they feared social unrest, and they wanted greater respect for the church and the army. To many of his enemies, Blum was not a "real Frenchman" because he was a Jew. Even after the Popular Front was no longer in power, its opponents feared that it might soon run France again. As war with Germany approached, the anti-Popular Front Frenchmen coined a slogan: "Better Hitler than Blum."

The Jews of France

To most European Jews, however, France remained a country worthy of admiration. Thousands of Jews moved to France from eastern Europe in the 1920s and 1930s. By 1933, when Hitler rose to power in Germany, there were already over 100,000 foreign-born Jews in France, some of whom by this time were French citizens.

Two very different Jewish communities had formed in France by 1939. About 150,000 people made up the "old" Jewish population of France. They did not even call themselves "Jews" (or *Juifs* in French). Instead, they usually used the word "Israelite" to describe themselves. They were generally prosperous, working in law, medicine, and other lucrative professions, and in business. Except for their religion—which many did not practice very strictly—they were very similar to the non-Jewish French people among whom they lived and worked.

The eastern European Jews who had settled in France were generally not as well off as the "old" Jewish elite. Most were workers or had small businesses, especially in the clothing industry. Many spoke Yiddish to each other rather than French. They were often members of political organizations that they had supported before arriving in France. The eastern European Jews of France were more likely to live in a neighborhood with other Jews than were the Jews who had been born in France. Much of the antisemitism in France in the 1930s was aimed at these so-called "foreign" Jews rather than at the "French" Israelites.

From 1933 until the beginning of World War II in 1939, another 50,000 Jews fled to France from Germany, Austria, and what is now the Czech Republic—areas of Europe that Hitler took over. Very few of these Jews were French citizens; since the Nazis had taken away the Jews' right to citizenship, the Jewish people were considered "stateless"—people who had no legal citizenship anywhere. In the late 1930s, Poland

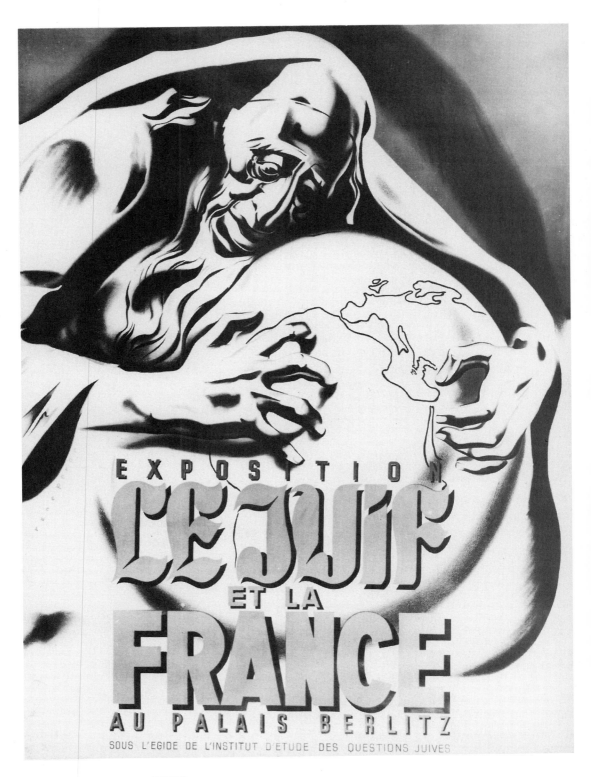

EXPOSITION
LE JUIF
ET LA
FRANCE
AU PALAIS BERLITZ
SOUS L'EGIDE DE L'INSTITUT D'ETUDE DES QUESTIONS JUIVES

A French antisemitic
propaganda poster asking the
French people to expose the
Jews for trying to take over
the world.

The Man Who Saved Ten Thousand Jews

As the refugees from northern France headed south, many tried to escape the country altogether. To leave legally, they needed a document, called a visa, issued by the country in which they were going to settle. In Bordeaux, a French port on the Atlantic coast, thousands of refugees were desperate to obtain these documents so they could board ships leaving the country. They tried to get them from the foreign consulates in Bordeaux. (A consulate is a diplomatic office that looks after the needs of a country's citizens in a foreign city. For example, the consulate might help arrange business deals between companies in the two countries or help one of its citizens who has been arrested.)

The counsel-general of Portugal was Aristides de Sousa Mendes, a lawyer by profession and a deeply religious Catholic. He began to issue huge numbers of Portuguese transit visas to the French refugees, including Jews. The Portuguese government, although it was neutral in the war, was friendly to Germany. It ordered Sousa Mendes to stop, but he continued to issue the documents. From June 17 to June 19, 1940, Sousa Mendes issued 30,000 transit visas, 10,000 of them to Jews.

For these actions, Sousa Mendes was arrested and sent back from Bordeaux to Portugal, where he lost his job and his pension and was barred from practicing law. He died in poverty in 1954. He said that he had disobeyed his government's orders because he acted as a Christian. Some of his own ancestors were Portuguese Jews who had been forced to convert to Catholicism back in 1497. More than ten years after his death, he was honored by Israel as one of "the Righteous Among the Nations," a non-Jew who had acted to save Jews. In 1987, the Portuguese government officially named him a hero. Sousa Mendes probably saved more Jews from the Holocaust than any single individual except Raoul Wallenberg. (See section on Wallenberg in Chapter 12, pp. 347–49.)

and some other eastern European countries also passed laws that stripped away the citizenship of Jews, so some of the Jews who migrated to France from eastern Europe were also "stateless." (Despite this, many thousands of "foreign" Jewish

World War I hero Marshal Phillippe Pétain was chosen to head the French Vichy government. He was more sympathetic to the Nazis than to the French Communists.

men volunteered for the French army to fight against Nazi Germany when the war began.) In addition, between 25,000 and 50,000 Jewish refugees (people who flee to a foreign country to escape danger or persecution) from the Netherlands and especially from Belgium poured into France in the spring of 1940 as the German army overran their countries.

Most Jews in France, both French-born and foreign-born, lived in the northern and eastern parts of the country, especially in the city of Paris. There were also large Jewish communities in Alsace and Lorraine, the eastern French provinces that had been part of the German empire from 1871 to 1918 and became part of Germany during World War II (1939–45).

War and Defeat

France was considered the greatest military power in Europe when World War II broke out. Although Germany had quickly conquered Poland, Denmark, the Netherlands, and Belgium, no one thought that defeating France would be so easy. Yet, the French army and its British ally were badly beaten by the attack of the German armored divisions. In six weeks of heavy fighting, the Germans smashed the French army, forced the British to evacuate and send their army back to England, and closed in on Paris.

As the French government fled from Paris, chaos grew. Four million civilians clogged the roads heading south to escape the advancing Germans. Among them were thousands of Jews, including approximately 50,000 "foreign" Jews.

Marshal Phillippe Pétain, a hero of World War I (1914–18), was chosen to head the new government in France. Pétain had helped defeat the Germans in 1918, but now he was an old man of 84. He had more sympathy for the ideas of the Nazis than he did for the ideas of the Popular Front. As historian Nora Levin put it, "More than Nazism, Pétain despised and feared democracy."

Pétain quickly agreed to an armistice (truce) with Germany to stop the fighting. France was divided into two parts. The northern half and all of the Atlantic coast were occupied by the German army. The southern part of the country was controlled by Pétain's French government. The new French government's laws also applied to the German-occupied zone—but only if they did not interfere with German orders. France would have to pay for the huge cost of the German occupation, millions of dollars a day. Germany refused to release French soldiers taken prisoner in the battle.

Vichy France

Pétain's French government made its new capital at Vichy (pronounced "VEE-SHE"), a small city in central France famous for its mineral water and baths. Vichy was chosen because it had many hotels that could be used as government offices. The "unoccupied" zone of France become known as "Vichy France," and the government was referred to as "Vichy." The town was soon swarming with the politicians who had opposed the Popular Front. The French constitution was changed to abolish democracy. Pétain was given dictatorial powers as the head of the new "French State," which replaced the French Republic. Even the famous slogan of the republic, dating back to the French Revolution, was changed. Instead of "Liberty, Equality, Fraternity" (brotherhood), the Vichy government's slogan was "Work, Family, Country."

Some French people opposed Vichy from the beginning. Charles de Gaulle, a little-known French army general, fled to London and declared that France should continue to fight Germany. With British support, he organized French forces that had escaped the country to continue the war alongside the British. They were called "the Free French," and eventually they would fight in Africa, Italy, France, and Germany itself. De Gaulle's goal—which he largely achieved—was for Britain and later for the other Allies that joined the war against Germany (the United States and the Soviet Union) to treat the Free French as the real government of France.

Little-known army general Charles de Gaulle maintained that France should continue to fight Germany. He declared the Free French as the real government of France.

Inside France, both in the occupied zone and in Vichy France, networks of resistance groups began to surface. They published illegal newspapers, hid people whom the Nazis were trying to arrest, and attempted to organize opposition to Vichy. Although they were often small and loosely organized at first, these groups eventually grew quite large and engaged in a wide variety of actions. They forged identity papers and other documents needed for Jews to survive in occupied France; used secret radios to send reports on German military forces to England; hid British and American airmen whose planes were shot down over France; attacked German troops; blew up railroad lines; and committed other acts of sabotage, (obstructing German military actions and destroying its equipment). Jews played an important part in many of these resistance organizations. It is estimated that 15 to 20 percent of the active resistance members were Jews, even though the Jewish people made up less than 1 percent of the population. In addition, there were several all-Jewish resistance groups.

But most French people were not active in the resistance—certainly not at the beginning. The few pro-Nazi French were happy that France had been defeated by Germany and many more agreed with the Vichy government about the way France should be run. These groups supported a policy of cooperation with Germany. Probably more French people, however, took a "wait and see" attitude. They respected Pétain and thought he would do his best for France in a difficult situation. These middle-of-the-road French citizens did not support the Germans who had conquered their country, nor did they share the Nazis' ideas. They were simply trying to continue to live their own lives as best they could. Average French citizens needed to work, earn a living, and send their children to school. They hoped Vichy would be able to arrange for the release of the 2 million French prisoners of war held in Germany. They also hoped Pétain could ease the harsh conditions the Germans were imposing on their country. Perhaps most of all, though, they hoped that the war was over for France.

Collaboration

At the beginning of the occupation, when it looked almost certain that Germany would win the war, many French leaders thought that France's future—and their own

personal power—depended on developing a close relationship with Germany. They wanted to collaborate with Germany. "Collaboration" means working together, but the act of "collaborating" soon took on a far different meaning. Many French people could understand that France's back was up against a wall: the country often *had* to do what Germany wanted. After all, there were 3 million German soldiers occupying France.

But the idea of voluntary collaboration with the Nazis was too much to take. The French population was outraged by the official publication of news photographs of Pétain greeting Hitler as a friend. And Pierre Laval, the most powerful Vichy leader, openly said that he hoped Germany would win the war. As time went on, more and more French citizens thought that Laval and his fellow collaborators were traitors.

In fact, Vichy cooperated with Germany more than the governments of most other occupied countries, even though

A group of French women who collaborated with the Germans are driven through Cherbourg, France, on the back of a truck in July 1944. Their heads were shaved as a form of punishment.

it had more bargaining power. France controlled most of North Africa, which included regions that were important in the war between Britain and Germany. French troops and administrators in North Africa and in other French colonies were still obeying the orders of the Vichy government. Vichy also controlled the powerful French fleet, which the Germans wanted to keep separate from the British navy. (The union of these forces would prove to be a powerful water-based enemy to the Germans.) Still, the Vichy government never really used these powerful advantages to bargain with the Germans.

Most of Germany's goals clashed with the economic interests of the people of France. The Germans wanted to secure money from the French government, to take over many French companies, and to buy French products cheaply. They also wanted access to the crops grown on French farms. Before long, they were demanding that French people be sent to Germany to work. And, as was the policy everywhere in German-occupied Europe, they wanted to kill the nation's Jews. Some Vichy leaders believed that by helping the Germans attack the Jews, they could gain the favor of the German government without becoming unpopular with the rest of the French people. For these leaders, it seemed easier to help the Nazis by being anti-Jewish than by giving in to any of Germany's other demands.

Vichy attack the Jews

In fact, Vichy began to attack the Jews even before the Germans asked them to do so. Only two months after the armistice, Vichy repealed the law that made it a crime to attack a group because of race or religion. Then, in October 1940, the first specifically anti-Jewish law was passed. It banned Jews from all government jobs, teaching positions, and the armed forces. The number of Jews in many other professions was restricted. The law defined Jews according to how many Jewish grandparents a person had, just as the Nazis had done. (See pp. 70–71.) This meant that a person of Jewish ancestry whose parents had become Catholics—and who had been raised Catholic—was still considered a Jew. In other words, the law treated the Jews as members of a different "race," not just a different religion. This 1940 decree marked the first time a racially based law had ever been put into effect in modern France.

The most terrible parts of the law applied to the "state-less" Jewish refugees, for it took away all their legal rights and made them subject to arrest. Soon 25,000 refugees from Germany, Austria, and the Czech lands were placed in detention camps by French police. They were forced to live under terrible conditions, with little protection from the cold. In some of the camps, people starved to death. There were cases of brutality by the French guards. Other Jews were later put into forced-labor groups. Their only crime was that they were Jews who had gone to France to escape persecution.

In March 1941, Vichy created a special government department in charge of Jewish affairs. The head of the department was a notorious anti-Semite. Later, he was replaced by a man whose hatred of Jews was even more violent. In June, the government ordered that property (such as businesses) belonging to Jews would be "Aryanized"—taken over and transferred to non-Jews. (Aryan was the term the Nazis used to refer to white Europeans with certain common ethnic charac-

Four female prisoners stand outside a barrack behind a barbed-wire fence at the Gurs transit camp in France, 1942.

teristics; Aryan as a "racial" category specifically excluded the Jews.) At the same time, all Jews were required to register with the government. These registration lists were then used by the Germans to seek out and arrest the area's Jews.

The occupied zone

The Germans were taking similar actions in their zone of France. In September 1940, Jews who had fled to southern France were barred by a German order from returning to their homes. Like most of the 4 million French people who had tried to escape to the south during the fighting, most of the Jews wanted to go home after the armistice. The German order forced them to stay in Vichy France and, strictly by chance, saved the lives of many Jews.

In April 1941, the Germans forbade Jews from making their livings at specified occupations—six months *after* Vichy had done so. A month later, Jews in occupied France were required to wear a six-pointed Jewish star at all times. The order applied to French-born Jews, not just "foreigners." It was extremely unpopular with most of the non-Jewish population, just as it was in Belgium and the Netherlands. Jewish war veterans wore the star alongside their military medals and paraded through the streets of Paris as crowds cheered them on. Vichy officials—even the leading anti-Semites— refused to extend the order to the Vichy zone.

That spring and summer, the Germans arrested almost 7,500 Jews. Most were foreigners, but the arrestees included 1,300 native-born French Jews. In December 1941, when the resistance tried to kill a German air force officer, the Germans arrested and later deported 1,000 French Jews. Most of them were doctors and lawyers. They imposed an enormous "fine" of a billion francs on the Jewish community. In addition, the Germans shot 95 hostages, 59 of them Jews. Throughout the occupation, the Germans took civilian hostages and executed them in large numbers whenever the resistance attacked German troops. A high proportion of Jews were always included among the hostages.

As time passed, the Germans arrested more and more Jews. At first the prisoners were sent to various camps, one of which was at Drancy, a suburb of Paris. There, an unfinished low-income housing project had been turned into a detention camp. For much of its history, Drancy was run and guarded by French police, not by the Germans.

Eventually, Drancy became the Nazis' transit camp, or stopover point, for all of France. Jews from all over the country were brought there. They usually stayed until transportation became available. Then, the Germans packed them into trains of locked cattle cars, about 1,000 people on each train, and sent them to "the east" for "resettlement." This transport cycle was essential to the realization of the Nazi's "Final Solution"—the Nazi code for the physical elimination of all European Jews. From March 1942 until July 1944, almost 78,000 Jews—many thousands of them children—left Drancy on these trains. Fewer than 3,000 ever came back. The main destination was Auschwitz, where almost all captives were killed in Nazi gas chambers. (See Chapter 9.)

The Nazi organization in charge of murdering the Jews of Europe was the *Schutzstaffel*, or the SS. The SS was the black-uniformed "security" force of the Nazi Party that was made up of the most dedicated Nazis. The SS intended to arrest and deport all the Jews of France, one trainload at a time—15,000 people a month. They would begin with the occupied zone. But to arrest this number of people they needed the cooperation of the French forces. The SS had only 3,000 police in all of France, and the German army refused to allow soldiers to take part in the roundup of the Jews. (The army was involved, however, in the seemingly random shooting of civilian hostages.)

At first, Vichy officials would not agree to allow the use of the French police for the Jewish arrests. The SS threatened to arrest and deport *all* Jews, including French citizens, if the French did not help. If Vichy ordered its police to cooperate, however, the SS promised that it would arrest only the "foreign" Jews. Pierre Laval, who was at this point running the Vichy government, agreed.

The Vel' d'Hiv'

The SS moved quickly to gather the foreign Jews of Paris for deportation. On July 16, 1942, they arrested 12,500 people, only half the number they had planned to capture that day. Single men without families were taken directly to Drancy and from there were sent to Auschwitz.

But the Germans had not yet authorized the deportation of small children from France. So families with children were taken to the Vélodrome d'Hiver, a glass-enclosed sports arena in Paris used for indoor bicycle races. (It was called the Vel' d'Hiv' [pronounced "Vel-deeve"] for short.) The French authorities had made no preparations for these prisoners. Guarded by French police, more than 8,000 people, including 4,000 children, slept on the ground or on the bleacher-type seats. They were stuck there with almost no food, little water, and inadequate sanitation. The heat and the smell were said to be unbearable. Some people went crazy, and several even committed suicide. Childhood diseases like measles spread quickly. The only medical care was provided by volunteers. Several women gave birth to babies under these terrible conditions. Some of the prisoners remained at the Vel' d'Hiv' for nearly a week. A few escaped when French policemen "looked the other way."

Buses then took the Jews to two detention camps about 50 miles south of Paris. Some of the Jews stayed in these camps for two more weeks, some for three. The adults and the older children were then marched to the railroad station in a nearby town. The French *gendarmes* (policemen) who guarded the camps had to use clubs and water hoses to separate the parents from their younger children, who were left behind.

The adults and the teenagers were packed onto a train. Four of these trains left the camps from the end of July through the first week of August 1942. The trains went to Auschwitz. At the end of the war, out of the more than 4,000 people in these transports, only 35 were still alive.

The smaller children, some too young to know their own names, remained at the camps. A small group of Red Cross volunteers and mothers who had not been deported took care of 3,500 children. Then the children were taken to the train station and sent to Drancy. They were told they would be reunited with their parents. Adult prisoners at Drancy tried to take care of them as well as they could. In the second half of August, the children were taken from Drancy on seven different trains. Like their parents and their older brothers and sisters before them, they were sent to Auschwitz. None survived.

The line that Vichy would not cross

The SS never intended to limit the Final Solution in France to foreign Jews. This was only a temporary compromise to gain the cooperation of the Vichy government. They were soon putting pressure on Vichy to arrest Jews who were French citizens, but Vichy would not agree. The SS was falling far behind its "schedule" for deporting Jews from France. In an effort to raise the number of deportees, the SS tried to convince Vichy to take away the citizenship of Jews who had not been born in France. If successful, this action would have made thousands more Jews into "foreigners" and therefore subject to deportation. But Vichy kept stalling. At one point, Laval agreed to one version of a law to strip some Jews of their citizenship. The SS prepared to arrest and deport more Jews. But a month later, Laval told the Germans that he had changed his mind—that he had not understood that the Jews would be deported. Another time, Laval even claimed he had lost his copy of the German proposals and would need a new one.

Pierre Laval, head of the Vichy government beginning in April 1942, claimed he only pretended to cooperate with the Germans, though his and some of the other Vichy leaders' actions prove otherwise.

Although the Germans sometimes arrested and deported Jews who were French citizens, including those born in France, they were never able to obtain Vichy's assistance in the task. Without the French government's help, the SS had a much more difficult job tracking down Jews. So the great majority of the Jews who were deported from France and killed in the Holocaust were foreign-born.

After the war, Laval tried to justify his actions. His first duty, he wrote, was "to my fellow countrymen of Jewish extraction." He claimed that he had to sacrifice the foreign Jews to save those who were French citizens. He admitted that this violated France's duty to those who had sought its protection. But, he asked, "How could it be otherwise in a country that was occupied by the German Army?"

Laval and other Vichy leaders claimed that they had played a "double game" against the Germans. Laval said that

Guilty Knowledge

After World War II ended, many of France's collaborators maintained that they had no knowledge of the fate of the Jews. They claimed to be completely ignorant of the fact that Jews were being sent to their deaths. It is quite possible that they did not know the exact details of what was happening, especially at first. But even if they knew nothing about the gas chambers, they certainly understood that the Nazis were treating the Jews with terrible brutality and that thousands of them were dying. They knew that they were helping to deport people who had lived and worked legally in France for many years, who had raised their families there, and who had sought French protection. They knew that they were helping to deport children because—and only because—they were Jewish.

Even the uncertainty about the Nazi plans was true only for a short while. Unlike ordinary people in Europe, including the Jews, Vichy officials had many ways of finding out what was really happening in other countries. Soon, rumors and then hard facts about the death camps reached the Vichy government through various sources. But Vichy continued to collaborate. Historians agree that by then, if any of the leaders of Vichy did not know what was happening, it was because they did not *want* to know.

he had pretended to cooperate, while always trying to give up as little as possible. But Laval and the others could not escape the fact that they had passed anti-Jewish laws on their own, without pressure from the Germans. They had helped the Nazis deport tens of thousands of people, including children, knowing they were sending them to die. (Vichy officials first suggested that the children of foreign Jews should also be deported.) They had organized special pro-Nazi units to hunt down members of the French resistance. The Danish and Dutch governments, though far weaker, had refused to do any of these things.

In part, the men of Vichy did what they did simply to keep their positions of power. They wanted to destroy

Responsibility and Apologies: The Police

For many years after World War II, there was not much discussion in France about the role of the French police in the Holocaust. Part of the reason is that in August 1944, the police played a major part in the armed uprising of the French resistance against the Germans in Paris. For many people, those few days of fighting changed the "image" of the police. Instead of an organization that had always collaborated with the Germans, the police were seen as fellow resistance fighters. In recent years, though, more and more people have recognized the involvement of the police in the brutal reality of the Holocaust. In 1997, the French police union issued an apology for these actions.

France's democratic tradition and permanently restructure the country, making it into a place where people obeyed the voice of authority. To achieve these goals, they were willing to collaborate with Nazi Germany, the most murderous government that had ever existed. And yet, even these men would not help kill those Jews they considered French. This was a line that Laval and his Vichy officials would not cross.

Historians describe Laval throughout his long political career as a clever and sneaky man, always looking for a way to get ahead, always making deals. In his version of the truth, the deal he made with the Germans saved the lives of thousands of French Jews. The price he paid was to cooperate in the murder of thousands of others. Almost all experts on the Holocaust reject Laval's argument. They believe that if Vichy had tried to protect *all* the Jews, if it had refused to cooperate with the arrests and deportations, fewer Jews would have died.

The French police

The giant raids to find Jews for deportation in Paris were conducted mainly by the French police under German supervision. This pattern continued throughout the occupation.

The record of the French police during the occupation is complex. On the one hand, they followed their orders and participated in the roundups of Jews. They supplied the manpower needed to carry out these operations. The cooperation of the French police was vital because they knew the neighborhoods and towns. Sometimes they were extremely efficient, searching carefully for hidden Jews. Sometimes, history tells us, they were as brutal as the Germans.

On the other hand, there are many examples of French police officers warning Jews before a raid—or purposely failing to find them. In the Paris raid of July 16, 1942, half the Jews targeted for arrest could not be found. Almost certainly, this was because word of the operation had been leaked by the French police. Sometimes the police would be sent to arrest a Jewish family and would instead tell them that they should pack a suitcase. Then the officers would leave, saying they would be back in an hour. No one was surprised if the family was gone when the police returned. Other times, the police simply accepted the word of neighbors that the family had already left town.

Vichy's role changes

The first arrests and deportations of the Jews in France occurred in the occupied zone. But around the same time that the children from the Vel' d'Hiv' were being sent to die at Auschwitz, the first Jews from the Vichy zone—those refugees who had been arrested by Vichy and held in detention camps for more than a year—were also being shuttled to the death camps. In August and September 1942, 10,000 Jewish refugees were turned over to the Nazis with the aid of French officials. The French further assisted the Germans by arranging for the children of "stateless" Jews to be deported along with their parents.

In November 1942, British and American troops landed in French North Africa to fight the Germans. Control of North Africa had been one of Vichy's most important bargaining weapons, and now it was gone. Within days, the German army crossed into the Vichy zone of France and occupied the whole country except for the southeastern corner. For the next year and a half, until the Germans were driven from France, they had direct control of most of the country. The Vichy government still existed, but it became more and

more of a puppet government whose actions were controlled by Germany.

The German effort to capture Jews increased, but these efforts were largely unsuccessful. More Jews were hiding, and a growing number of non-Jewish French people were protecting them. As the resistance increased in strength and the Allied armies won more and more battles against Germany, many collaborators became increasingly cautious. In some cases, officials who had cooperated with the Nazis earlier in the occupation were now working secretly with the resistance. At the same time, special pro-Nazi units of French volunteers, called the Milice ("Militia"), sided with the SS. Before long, the Milice and the resistance were fighting what amounted to a civil war.

Desperate to fulfill their quotas of French Jews destined for Auschwitz, the SS raided the children's homes that had been set up to care for children of deported Jews. They also

Jewish children liberated at Auschwitz pose in concentration camp uniforms between two rows of barbed wire. Children were sent to the camps not for political reasons, but only because they were Jewish.

American troops landing on the beaches of Normandy, France, on June 6, 1944, D-Day.

raided homes for the aged and swept through detention camps looking for Jews—without warning the Vichy authorities, whom they no longer trusted.

A reign of terror in Nice

The Germans put tremendous pressure on Italy to allow the arrest of Jews in the Italian-occupied zone of France. When Italy surrendered to the Allies in mid-1943, the SS swept into the area to try to capture the thousands of Jews who had sought Italian protection. The main SS target was Nice (pronounced "Nees"), the southern French resort city in the Italian zone. The roundup should have been easy. Jews in Nice had not been in hiding and had not needed false identity papers. Among them were many foreigners, who dressed differently or spoke French with an obvious accent.

But this time the SS didn't have the lists of names and addresses that Vichy had prepared for earlier roundups. They also lacked the assistance of the French police. The SS cruised the city in unmarked cars, grabbing pedestrians off the streets to check their identity papers. There were nightly raids on hotels and boardinghouses. They searched every train and bus that left the city and offered large rewards to informers who told them where to find Jews. Despite all these measures, the SS was able to capture fewer than 2,000 Jews out of the 25,000 to 30,000 known to be in the area.

The final months

On June 6, 1944, now known as D-Day, the British and American armies landed on the beaches of Normandy in northern France. After heavy fighting, they began to drive the Germans back. Resistance groups throughout France attacked the German forces. The Allies landed a second army in southern France. In late August, the tanks of de Gaulle's Free French forces, part of the Allied army that had fought its way eastward from Normandy, entered Paris. Resistance forces there had launched a full-scale uprising. By winter, the German troops were pushed back to their own border. France was free.

Throughout those final months of World War II, the SS never gave up its plan to kill the Jews. Trains left Drancy, bound for Auschwitz, until the Allied bombing of the French railroads and the sabotage of the resistance made railroad travel utterly impossible. The SS tried frantically to deport Jews from France even when the German army needed the trains for military purposes. When the Allied troops reached Paris and Drancy, the Nazis scrambled to send captives directly to the death camps from other places. More hostages, including many Jews, were executed. People who lingered in prisons for months were shot. Even if they lost the war against the Allies, the Nazis were determined to win their war against the Jews.

France and Vichy

To many French people, including de Gaulle and those who fought in the resistance, Vichy was never the real government of France—it was merely a gang of criminals that had taken over the country with German help. The opponents of Vichy felt that they alone represented the *real France.* Because of this, they did not believe that France—the real France, that is—had to apologize to anyone for anything. *France* did not help the Germans deport and murder Jews, only Vichy did.

Everyone knew and readily admitted that many individual French people had helped the Germans. Immediately after the German retreat, several thousand of the worst collaborators were tried by special resistance-run courts and executed. Members of the Milice were shot by firing squads with little attention to legal formalities. Pierre Laval was executed after a trial. Pétain was sentenced to death, but his sentence was changed to life imprisonment because of his age and his service to France during World War I.

As things settled down in postwar Europe, a myth began to develop in France that the great majority of the French had supported the resistance and only a small minority had ever sided with Vichy. People came to believe that the number of active collaborators was very small and that many of them—if not most—had already been punished by the resistance. This myth of noncompliance with the Nazis helped to restore pride in France after defeat and occupation by the Germans, and it was a way of trying to end the civil war between the supporters of Vichy and the resistance. The myth that almost all the collaborators had been punished allowed the French to try to close this chapter in their history.

Myths like these can help a country heal in the aftermath of tragedy, but such a serious distortion of reality can also be damaging. For years after the war, many French people hid their pasts. Some had helped the Nazis to deport Jews. Some had informed the Milice that Jews were hiding in their villages. These people were, just as the myth said, a small minority. But many more had supported Vichy, especially at the beginning. As a young man, even François Mitterrand, the president of France from 1981 to 1995, had held low-level jobs in the Vichy government and had supported Pétain before becoming a member of the resistance. A large number of French people had actually approved of the anti-Jewish laws that their country enacted. And millions of others who thought these laws were wrong and unjust had kept silent and had done nothing.

For Jews especially, the official attitude of France was unacceptable. They believed that *France,* not just a few

Frenchmen, had to claim some responsibility for the deaths of almost 80,000 people. In 1995, a half-century after the end of the Holocaust, president Jacques Chirac, who was too young to have played any part in those years, officially acknowledged France's part in the Nazi-organized attacks on the Jews.

Foreigners and Frenchmen

All together, about 78,000 Jews who had been in France died in the Holocaust. About 55,000 of the victims were foreigners. The other 23,000 were French citizens, including about 8,000 immigrants who had become citizens and another 8,000 children born in France to foreign parents. (Vichy always treated these French-born children as foreigners.) But Vichy could claim it had succeeded in saving all but 6,500 of the old Jewish community of France, the "Israelites."

A different point of view was expressed by Jules-Gérard Saliège, the Catholic archbishop of the southern French city of Toulouse. When Vichy turned over the stateless Jews from French detention camps to the Germans for deportation, he wrote a letter of protest and ordered all his priests to read it during Sunday Mass on August 23, 1942. Part of the letter reads as follows:

> Jews are men and women. Foreigners are men and women. All is not permitted against them, against these men, these women, these fathers and mothers. They are part of the human race.

12

Germany's Allies and the Jews:
Italy and Hungary

Italy

Italy was Germany's most important ally in Europe. It had been ruled by a dictator, Benito Mussolini, since 1922. In many ways, Mussolini and his Fascist Party had been a model for Hitler before the Nazis rose to power in Germany. Fascism is a system of government dominated by a single, all-powerful leader; fascist philosophy is very nationalistic and authoritarian, glorifying the state and giving it supreme powers over its people. The Nazi storm troopers, often called "brownshirts" because of their uniforms, were originally modeled on Mussolini's "Black Shirts," the thugs who beat up opponents of the Fascists. In fact, the Nazis and similar parties in other European countries were often called "Fascists."

The alliance with Hitler

Although there were many similarities between Mussolini's Fascist Italy and Adolf

Benito Mussolini and Adolf Hitler during Hitler's visit to Italy in 1938. Mussolini and his Fascist Party had been a model for Hitler before the Nazis came to power in Germany.

Hitler's Nazi Germany, there were also important differences. The Italian Fascists hardly ever talked about "racial" issues. There was very little mention of Jews, and they certainly were never portrayed as the main enemy of Italy. Jews constituted only one-tenth of 1 percent of the Italian population, and there was little antisemitism among the people. A few Jews even held important positions in the Fascist government in its early years.

After Hitler and the Nazis took over Germany, Italy and Germany became close allies. Italy sent troops and Germany sent airmen and planes to Spain to help the Fascist rebels who defeated Spain's elected government in a bloody civil war. Soon, however, it became clear that Germany, with its much greater economic and military power, was the "senior partner" and that Hitler—not Mussolini—was the leader of the Fascist movement in Europe.

Just before World War II (1939–45) began, Italy passed severe antisemitic laws modeled after those in effect in Germany. Although Mussolini had passed these laws in order to win favor with Hitler, his ally, he is said to have believed that "racial" theories were mere nonsense. His own sister was protecting Jews—and he knew it—but Mussolini felt this fact would only prove that Italy's antisemitic laws were meant to be "flexible." He did not mind that the Italian government sometimes failed to enforce the new laws very strictly. Italian officials were known to have readily accepted bribes from Jews, but, in general, evasion of the laws was greatly helped by the fact that very few Italians were antisemitic. Many Italians, even supporters of Mussolini, were embarrassed by the antisemitic decrees and did their best to make them less harsh.

Even so, the laws caused great pain for many Jews. Italian Jews lost their jobs and were driven into poverty. Jews in the Italian army, including generals, were forced to retire. Jews who had settled in Italy a short time before, including refugees from the Nazis, were especially hard-hit. Many—even those who had become Italian citizens—were forced to leave the country. Some were sent to prison camps, where they endured a miserable existence; others were moved to small towns, where they were forced to live under police supervision.

Temporary protection from deportation

While life was indeed difficult for the Jews of Italy, they were not being deported (forcibly removed from towns of residence) to death camps and killed. The Italians refused to allow Jews to be deported from the areas they controlled. Of all the countries occupied or strongly influenced by the Germans, only Italy protected not only its own Jews but foreign Jews within its own borders and even Jews in Italian-occupied areas of other countries.

In the part of southeastern France occupied by Italy, the Italian government allowed Jews to go about freely, even as

Jews being deported at an Italian transit camp. Jews in Italy fared better than most other European Jews during the Holocaust.

they were being rounded up by the Germans only a few miles away. Jews from the rest of France tried desperately to get to the Italian-controlled area where they would be safe. The Germans were furious and even sent high Nazi officials to Rome, Italy's capital, to demand that Mussolini do something about it. Mussolini promised to take care of the problem, but in fact the Italians did nothing to change their policy. In several cases, Italian troops even threatened to use force to prevent the French police, who were working for the Germans, from arresting Jews.

But the situation changed in the summer of 1943. As the British and American armies were invading Italy, Mussolini's government was overthrown. A new government took over Italy and surrendered to the Allied Powers. The German army rushed in to occupy the northern half of the country and continued its fight against the Allies. From then until the end of the war in May 1945, the Germans controlled much of

Italy directly. In the north, they set up a puppet government with Mussolini as its leader. Mussolini and his remaining Fascist supporters had little real power, but by this time they were cooperating with the Germans in every way, including in trying to arrest Jews. For 20 months, thousands of Jews were arrested and deported by the Germans with the help of Italian Fascists. Many Jews went into hiding, protected by non-Jewish Italians. A large percentage hid in the monasteries and convents of the Catholic Church.

The *Schutzstaffel,* or the SS, searched for the Jews throughout Italy; the citizens who hid them were taking a great risk. (The SS, also known as "blackshirts," was the military unit of the Nazi Party that was responsible for the elimination of the Jews of Europe.) Some historians feel that ordinary Italians were more willing to gamble with their own lives when it became clear that Germany was going to lose the war. But the actions of the Italians, even at the beginning of the war, show that most of the nation's people were genuinely concerned with the welfare of the Jews. Of the roughly 45,000 Jews who were still in Italy in 1943, about 8,000 died. Except for Denmark, this was a lower percentage than in any other area controlled by Germany.

Hungary

Before World War I (1914-18), Hungary was part of the Austrian Empire, which controlled much of central Europe. It was often called the Austro-Hungarian Empire because Hungary and Austria were the two nations that ran the Empire. The Hungarian part of the empire included many areas that were not part of the historic country of Hungary.

Hungary, like Austria and Germany, was one of the countries that lost the most in World War I. It became much smaller, forced to give up large areas that it had ruled. However, in some of these areas Hungarian-speaking people were large minorities, and sometimes even a majority. The desire to get these territories back was a major force in Hungarian politics from the end of World War I in 1918. There was much anger against the peace treaty that Hungary had signed with Britain and France that had taken these areas away. In these ways, Hungary was similar to Germany.

Hungarian antisemitism

As in Germany, there was an attempted communist revolution in Hungary right after World War I. Both the revolutionary government and the forces that defeated it were extremely violent. Antisemitism was common in Hungary and, just as in Germany, many Hungarians falsely blamed Jews both for the peace treaty and for the attempted communist take-over. There was a wave of bloody pogroms (anti-Jewish riots) in the early 1920s.

The government that came to power at this time continued to rule Hungary until almost the end of World War II. Its leader was Miklós (Nicholas) Horthy, who had been an admiral in the old Austro-Hungarian navy. His title was regent, which is someone who rules in place of a king, such as when the king is a child. But Hungary did not have a king, and Horthy was basically a dictator, a ruler with absolute authority, although opposition political parties and a parliament (legislature) continued to exist.

Miklós Horthy, Regent of Hungary, allied with Hitler to regain Hungarian territory lost after World War I.

Horthy's government was hostile to the Jews. Most Jews were dismissed from government jobs, and the number who could be admitted to universities was restricted. Although violence against Jews decreased after the pogroms, Hungarian citizens remembered how recently mobs had attacked the Jews.

In 1930, there were about 450,000 Jews in Hungary, about 5 percent of the population. About half of the Jews lived in the capital of Budapest, where they made up 20 percent of the population. Budapest's Jews were prominent in the arts, theater, and literary life. Many more were involved in business and commercial activities, where they played an important role in the Hungarian economy. This was partly because there were relatively few other middle-class people. Most Hungarians were still peasants, small farmers who lived on the land, but rarely owned it. The richest and most powerful people were great landowners, on whose land the peasants worked. As in several parts of eastern Europe, Jews filled the gap between the peasants and the landowners, who usually did not want to get involved in business activities. The importance of Jews in the economy made them more noticeable, and was probably one of the reasons that antisemitism was so strong in Hungary.

Many of the Jews of Budapest, much like Jews in western and northern Europe, lived, dressed, and spoke like their non-Jewish neighbors. A significant number of Jews, mostly in Budapest, had become Christians, partly because of Hungarian antisemitism. In the rest of the country, however, Hungarian Jews were often very traditional in the way they dressed and spoke, and many were extremely religious, strictly observing Jewish laws and customs.

Hungarian Jews would have faced many difficulties just because of the widespread antisemitism in their country and the attitude of the government. But their troubles became much worse because of something that had little connection to the Jews: Hungary's foreign alliances.

The German alliance

The Horthy government wanted an alliance with Germany. This was mainly because Germany and Hungary both wanted to change the borders created by the peace treaties after World War I. Both countries wanted to get back territories they had lost, but only Germany had the power to accomplish this. After the Nazis came to power in Germany in 1933, one of the ways for Hungary to stay friendly with Germany was to attack Jews. In addition, German influence on Hungarian life was increasing. There were violent Nazi-style organizations, such as the Arrow Cross, that sometimes supported the government, but also put pressure on it to move even closer to Nazi Germany and to increase anti-Jewish measures. The Nazi government helped finance these groups and spread antisemitic propaganda in Hungary.

Hungary passed its first anti-Jewish law in 1938. It limited the number of Jewish employees in private companies to 20 percent of the total. In 1939, a more drastic law restricted Jewish participation in newspaper and radio work, and prevented Jews from entering professions like medicine and law unless the number of Jews in these professions fell below 6 percent. Jews who were not born in Hungary could no longer become citizens. Even Jews born in Hungary lost the right to vote unless their families had lived in the country since 1868. The laws also defined Jews as a race, rather than a religion. This meant that even Jews who had become Christians would be affected. The Hungarian churches opposed these aspects of the laws, but they did not oppose discrimination against Jews who did not convert to Christianity.

At the time these laws were passed, Hungary's alliance with Nazi Germany began to succeed in getting Hungary the land that it wanted. In 1938, after Hitler threatened to go to war, Britain and France agreed to give Germany a section of Czechoslovakia, despite that country's protests. Hungary also got a section of the country, as a reward for its friendship with Hitler. The following year, when Germany destroyed Czechoslovakia completely, Hungary again received a part. Later, Hungary got a very large section of Romania (the area known as Transylvania) and part of Yugoslavia. All these areas had large Hungarian-speaking populations. They also had many Jews, almost a third of a million. There were now over 700,000 Jews under Hungarian rule. Except for Poland and the Soviet Union (Russia), this was now the largest Jewish population in Europe.

The return of Hungary's "lost" territories seemed like great successes for the country. But in return, Hungary became Hitler's ally. German troops were allowed to cross through Hungary when Germany invaded Yugoslavia, even though Hungary had signed a friendship treaty with Yugoslavia. Soon after, Hungary joined Germany in its invasion of the Soviet Union in June 1941. The price Hungary eventually paid for this alliance was enormous. Hundreds of thousands of Hungarian soldiers would die fighting in Russia, Hungary would be devastated by Allied bombs and invasion, and by the end of World War II, it would again lose all its new territory. The price paid by the Jews of Hungary for their country's alliance with Hitler was worse still.

Hungarian Jews in the first years of the war

In the first years of World War II, many able-bodied Jewish men were put into forced-labor brigades of the Hungarian army. (Jews were not allowed to be regular soldiers.) Eventually, about 130,000 Jews served in these units. When Hungary invaded the Soviet Union, 40,000 Jews in forced-labor brigades were sent to the front lines to accompany the Hungarian troops. They were treated with great brutality by the Hungarian army, given inadequate food and clothing, and subject to random shootings. About three-quarters of these men died from the cold, malnutrition, and execution.

In 1941, the Hungarian government rounded up and deported over 20,000 "stateless" Jews—people who were no longer citizens of any country. Several thousand were taken to be used as slave labor by the Hungarian army fighting in Ukraine and Russia. The rest were sent to a part of Ukraine then controlled by Germany, where they were massacred by one of the special Nazi murder units called *Einsatzgruppen*. (See Chapter 7, pp. 186-88.) In addition, Hungarian troops taking part in the Nazi invasion of Yugoslavia murdered 4,000 Jews there, as well as 6,000 non-Jewish Serbs. During these massacres, some Hungarian officers ordered Jews to be buried alive.

And yet, despite these events and the general anti-semitism of the Hungarian government, most Hungarian Jews were still alive in 1944. Regardless of German pressure, there had been no more deportations. Hungarian Jews had not been sent to the death camps in occupied Poland, as the Jews of almost every other country had. The Hungarian prime minister, Miklós Kállay, said publicly that he favored "resettlement" as the long-term solution to Hungary's "Jewish problem." But he made it clear that this could not happen until Germany explained exactly where the Jews were being resettled. As Kállay probably understood, the Nazis could not do this because the Jews were being murdered, not "resettled."

As long as the Hungarian Jews remained in Hungary, they were far better off than the Jews of the rest of Europe. The Soviet army, beating back Germany and its allies, was approaching the old Hungarian border, ready to drive towards Budapest. It looked like the great majority of Hungarian Jews would survive the war.

The Jews in danger

In March 1944, everything changed. Germany suspected—correctly—that the Hungarian government was trying to get out of the war, in order to avoid a Soviet invasion of Hungary. In addition, Hitler was furious that the Hungarian government refused to deport the Jews. He demanded that Horthy come to Germany for a meeting. When he did, he was taken prisoner by the Germans and not allowed to communicate with his government. When he was allowed to return to Budapest, 24 hours later, the Germans controlled Hungary.

Carrying out a carefully prepared plan, they had rushed troops into the country. German officials watched over every department of the Hungarian government. Kállay escaped to Turkey, while other political leaders who opposed Hungary's pro-German policies were arrested. Opposition political parties and newspapers were banned. The new government was made up of strong supporters of Germany, including many members of the Arrow Cross movement, the Hungarian Nazis. Instead of an ally, Hungary was now a puppet of Germany.

Adolf Eichmann supervised the deportation of the Hungarian Jews. He later proposed trading Jewish prisoners for trucks to use against the Soviets. The Western Allies rejected his plan.

Suddenly, the Jews of Hungary were in immediate danger. Along with the German troops who occupied the country, and the German officials who really ran the government, the Nazis also sent the "Jewish experts" of the SS into Budapest. They were led by Adolf Eichmann, the head of the "Jewish Affairs Section" of the RSHA, the German initials for the Main Office for Reich Security. The RSHA was in charge of the Holocaust, and Eichmann and his assistants had already supervised the deportation of millions of European Jews to the death-camps. (See Chapter 8.)

Eichmann and his men, with the help of their Hungarian supporters, acted much more quickly than they had in other countries. Like everyone else, they knew that it was only a matter of months before the Soviet army arrived. Within a month, Jews outside of Budapest were being forced to move into ghettos, special fenced-off sections of a town. People from small towns had to move to ghettos in a larger city. When all the Jews were concentrated in relatively few ghettos, it would be much easier to deport them. This was the pattern that the Nazis had followed in Poland earlier in the war. (See Chapters 5 and 6.)

Prisoners of the Auschwitz death camp unload the property of deported Hungarian Jews who were gassed upon their arrival.

Eichmann divided Hungary into six zones. The plan was to "clear" each zone of Jews, one zone at a time. Budapest would be last. The first trains, carrying Jews who had been arrested for changing their addresses without permission (that is, for trying to hide), left for the Auschwitz death camp by the end of April. The organized deportations from the first of Eichmann's zones began in the middle of May. Train after train carried thousands of Jews to Auschwitz, where almost all were immediately gassed. (See Chapter 9 for more information on Auschwitz.) By June 7, nearly 300,000 Jews had been deported. By July 7, the total was almost 440,000. It was less than four months since the Germans had taken over Hungary.

Military defeat and the Holocaust

As in other parts of German-controlled Europe, the approach of the Allied armies, and the growing certainty that Germany would lose the war, seemed to make the Nazis more determined than ever to kill the Jews. Even if Germany were defeated or even destroyed, the Nazis would make sure that they won their war against the Jews.

But at the same time, the desperate military situation meant that even some of the top Nazi leaders were also thinking about how to use the Jews to help prevent defeat and to preserve their own lives and positions. Some of them hoped to make peace with the two western Allies, Britain and the United States, while continuing to fight the Soviet Union. Some even believed that the British and Americans might join Germany in a war against the Communist Soviet Union.

These Nazi leaders saw that they would have to get rid of Hitler in order to make a deal. They realized that continuing the murder of the Jews would prevent a deal, but they thought that if they now offered to end the deportations and murders, the fact that they had already killed millions of people would be ignored. Although the Nazis' hopes for an alliance with Britain and America were completely unrealistic, they are the background to one of the strangest episodes of the Holocaust.

A million Jews for sale

At the same time as he was preparing for the deportations of hundreds of thousands of Jews, Eichmann was also offering to allow them to live. On April 25, 1944, Eichmann met with Joel Brand, a leader of the Council for Assistance and Rescue, an organization of Hungarian Jews known as the "Vaadah," the Hebrew word for "council." The Vaadah had operated for two years, helping to smuggle Jews from Poland and Slovakia into Hungary, providing them with false papers, collecting information on what the Germans were doing in Poland and other places. The Vaadah also had connections with the American Jewish Joint Distribution Committee, which helped finance rescue efforts in Europe.

"I suppose you know who I am," Eichmann told Brand, as recounted by Alex Weissberg in *Desperate Mission: Joel Brand's Story*. "I was in charge of the *aktions* [anti-Jewish operations] in Germany, Poland, and Czechoslovakia. Now it is Hungary's turn."

But Eichmann proposed a deal. "I am prepared to sell you one million Jews." Brand could take them from anywhere in Europe, even from Auschwitz. "Who do you want to

Allied Priorities

The rejection of Adolf Eichmann's deal to save 1,000,000 Jews has been a subject of great controversy ever since. Eichmann, the director of the "Jewish Affairs Section" of the Main Office of Reich Security, proposed to the western Allies, the United States and Britain, that Germany would exchange 1,000,000 Jewish prisoners for goods and trucks to be used only against the Soviet army. The British thought the offer was part of an effort to create a split between the Soviet Union and the western Allies. This was almost certainly part of the reason the offer was made. Top Nazi leaders were trying to establish secret contacts with British and American representatives, hoping that a split among the Allies would save them from defeat. They were convinced—right to the end of the war—that the Allies would not stick together. The Allies understood this, and were determined to maintain unity until Germany had surrendered unconditionally.

However, this does not completely explain the way the British treated Joel Brand, the leader of the Council for Assistance and Rescue whom Eichmann approached with his proposal. By the time Eichmann's offer was rejected, the British knew that the Nazis had already murdered millions of Jews. They knew about Auschwitz and its gas chambers. They knew that the largest remaining Jewish population in Europe, the Jews of Hungary, were being deported to Auschwitz. While Brand was on his mission to the British, Jewish leaders were also urging the British and Americans to bomb the railroad lines from Hungary to Auschwitz, and to bomb the death camp itself. These ideas were not treated as high priorities, despite the warnings of the Jewish leaders that every day was crucial. The British and American air forces eventually rejected these proposals, saying there were too many technical difficulties.

Many historians have argued that bombing Auschwitz and the rail lines leading to it would have been possible. They point out that there were in fact air raids near Auschwitz around this time, though they were aimed at other targets nearby. Other historians defend the Allied decision. They say that it would not have been possible to bomb Auschwitz without killing thousands of prisoners. Bombing the railroad lines, they say, would have had very little effect, because they could be repaired quickly and alternate routes could have been used in the meantime.

It is clear that the Allied leaders had decided that winning the war against Germany as quickly as possible was more important than any other consideration. They would not use their air forces for anything that might delay their military objectives. They would not even seriously consider any proposal that was aimed directly at rescuing the Jews, rather than defeating Germany militarily. They believed the best way to stop the Nazi murder of the Jews was to defeat Germany. But the Allied victory would come too late to save most of the Jews of Hungary.

save?" Eichmann asked. "Young men, young women, old people, children? Sit down and talk."

Eichmann did not want money. He wanted goods, including soap, coffee, tea, and chocolate. Most important, he wanted 10,000 trucks. He promised that the trucks would be used only against the Soviet army, not the British and Americans. "Goods for blood, blood for goods," he told Brand. Brand would go to Istanbul, in Turkey, and try to make the arrangements. "If you come back from Istanbul and tell me the offer has been accepted, I will close Auschwitz." Then, Eichmann said, he would bring 100,000 Jews to a safe border. When he received the first 1,000 trucks, he would release another 100,000 Jews. "We'll go on like that. A thousand trucks for every hundred thousand Jews."

In Istanbul, Brand met with representatives of Jewish organizations and of the British government. It was soon clear that the British and Americans would never allow trucks to be sent to the German army to use against the Soviets. Brand hoped he would be able to get Eichmann to accept money instead.

Discussions and negotiations between Brand and the British went on and on, even though Eichmann had made it clear that his offer was only good for a short time. The mass deportations from Hungary to Auschwitz were soon under way. When Brand tried to travel to Syria to meet with other officials, the British arrested him, and kept him in custody. Then, in mid-July, they publicly announced their rejection of Eichmann's secret offer, calling it a mixture of blackmail and threats. By then, more than half the Jews of Hungary were dead.

Raoul Wallenberg

By early July 1944, the Jews from all the zones of Hungary except Budapest had been deported to Auschwitz. Over 400,000 had been sent on the trains. A complicated set of factors now temporarily stopped the deportations. Heinrich Himmler, head of all Nazi security forces, including those responsible for carrying out the killings of the Holocaust, was trying to negotiate for an end to the war with the Americans and British without Hitler's knowledge. The Hungarian government maneuvered to get out of the war as the Soviet army invaded. In addition, the secrecy that had surrounded the Holocaust was now almost completely gone. The leaders of every country knew that the Nazis were not just deporting and persecuting the Jews, but were trying to exterminate

Raoul Wallenberg saved the lives of tens of thousands of Hungarian Jews. He died of a heart attack in a Soviet prison in 1947.

them. At this time, a hero appeared to save the Jews remaining in Budapest.

His name was Raoul Wallenberg. He was a Swedish diplomat, a member of one of the richest families in Sweden, and a relative of the royal family. He had many connections with the United States, where he had attended the University of Michigan. Wallenberg went to Budapest in July, supposedly as a representative of neutral Sweden. In fact, he was there specifically to try to save the Jews.

Wallenberg began by issuing Swedish passports to any Hungarian Jews who had relatives or business contacts in Sweden. Then he began issuing "protective passports" to other Jews, putting them under the protection of the Swedish government. Soon, diplomats from other neutral countries such as Switzerland, Portugal, and Spain also issued protective documents, as did the representative of Pope Pius XII. Wallenberg eventually rented 30 buildings, put Swedish flags on them, and declared them to be Swedish territory, like a foreign embassy. Then he used the buildings to house as many Jews as he could. Fifteen thousand people lived in these buildings, in what became known as the "international ghetto," protected by the Swedish flag.

Two hundred thousand Jews remained in the Hungarian capital. Despite Himmler's wishes to end the deportations, Eichmann was determined to send them to their deaths. He could no longer deport them to Auschwitz, which the Nazis would soon begin to dismantle. (See Chapter 9, pp. 276–77.) Instead, Eichmann ordered that the Jews be rounded up and deported on foot. In November 1944, the first of a series of death marches began. Around 30,000 people marched for seven days, with no food, through rain and snow, heading for the Austrian border. Guards shot anyone who could not keep up.

Wallenberg and his staff tried to free people from these marches. He claimed they were under Swedish protection. He threatened and bluffed, he pleaded, he bribed the Germans and Hungarians. Sometimes he succeeded. When the marches were called off, there were still 160,000 Jews alive in Budapest.

That winter, as Soviet artillery and Allied planes bombarded the starving city, the Arrow Cross (Hungarian Nazis) continued to murder Jews in Budapest, often torturing them first, then throwing their bodies in the River Danube. Another 20,000 Jews died. Even after the Soviet army entered Budapest in January 1945, the Arrow Cross killings continued in the areas of the city they still controlled. Finally, after almost a month of heavy fighting, the Soviet army completed its capture of the city.

On January 17, 1945, Raoul Wallenberg was on his way to a meeting with the Soviet military commander when he disappeared. The Soviet government first said he was under "Soviet protection," then denied any knowledge. Then an official Soviet newspaper said he must have been killed by the Germans or the Arrow Cross. In 1952, several released prisoners claimed they had seen Wallenberg in a Soviet prison. In 1957, the Soviet government announced that Wallenberg had died of a heart attack in a Soviet prison in 1947. But reports that he was still alive in prison continued for many years.

No one is sure what happened to Raoul Wallenberg, or why. There is some evidence that the Soviet authorities did not trust the Swedish diplomats in Budapest, apparently suspecting them of being German spies. Or the Soviet government may have been suspicious of Wallenberg because of his ties to the United States. But the terrible irony of his story is clear: the man who faced down the Nazis and saved tens of thousands of people, disappeared and died at the hands of the liberators.

13

Judgments

O n May 8, 1945, Nazi Germany surrendered unconditionally to the Allied armies. The Holocaust—when Adolf Hitler and his Nazi Party controlled Germany and tried to wipe out all the Jews of Europe—was over. Germany was divided into four zones, occupied by American, British, French, and Soviet (Russian) troops. The victorious Allies now had to decide what to do about their defeated enemy.

In the last weeks of World War II, ordinary people throughout the world began to learn what the Nazis had done. As Allied soldiers reached the concentration camps of Germany, they found the bodies or remains of thousands and thousands of victims, and thousands more alive, but only barely. As survivors and witnesses began to talk and as Nazi documents and records came to light, the enormous scale of the Nazi crimes became apparent.

What was to be done with the people responsible for these crimes? Adolf Hitler, the Führer and supreme leader of Nazi Germany, was dead. He had killed himself in his command bunker beneath the bombed-out ruins of Berlin as the Soviet army was raising its flag over the German capital. Josef Goebbels, who had run Hitler's propaganda machine, had also killed himself in Berlin, along with his wife and children. Heinrich Himmler, head of the terror machinery of the Nazi state, had tried to escape from the Allies, disguised as an ordinary soldier. When his identity was discovered, he had killed himself with hidden poison. Heinrich Müller, one-time head of the *Geheime Staatspolizei,* or the Gestapo (the German secret police), had disappeared.

Many others, leaders of the German government, of the Nazi Party, and of the German military, were still alive and in custody. Should they be treated as the leaders of any other defeated country? Nazi Germany was not just a normal country that had lost a war. Its leaders had planned and carried out the murder of millions of civilians, including nearly six million European Jews.

During the war, the Allies had made several public statements that the Nazis would be held responsible for their crimes and that, in fact, the punishment of these crimes was one of the aims of the war against Germany. Some individuals who had committed crimes had been brought to justice even before the war was over.

The first trials

The first trial for Nazi atrocities (horrible and cruel acts) occurred in the Soviet Union (Russia) in July 1943, while the Nazis still controlled most of Europe. In the recently recaptured city of Krasnodov, a Soviet military tribunal (special court of justice) had tried thirteen Soviet citizens for participating in *Einsatzgruppe* D, one of the "special-action groups" the Nazis formed to murder Jews and others during the invasion of the Soviet Union. (See Chapter 7, pp. 186-88.) *Einsatzgruppe* D had committed over seven thousand murders in Krasnodov, including killing every patient in the city hospital and the children's hospital.

In addition, the Soviets had tried members of the staff of the Majdanek extermination camp, in Eastern Poland, a few

Long piles of bodies found at the Bergen-Belsen concentration camp after British forces liberated it.

months after their troops freed it in July 1944. The Soviet army reached Majdanek before the Nazis could dismantle it and move the survivors to other camps, as happened later. The Soviets captured a great many records that the Germans did not have time to burn.

The Majdanek trial produced the first evidence of the carefully organized and systematic nature of Nazi killing. Many people, especially in the United States and Britain, found the stories of what had happened hard to believe and thought that the Soviets must be exaggerating. Later it became clear that the Majdanek evidence not only was true, but was only a small part of what the Nazis had done. With the facts unfolding countless horrors, the Allies came to believe that Nazi leaders had to be put on trial. They wanted the people of the world, including the people of Germany, to understand the scale of Nazi crimes.

In September 1945, a British military court tried SS guards from the Bergen-Belsen concentration camp, some of whom also had been at Auschwitz. (SS are the initials of *Schutzstaffel,* the Nazi Party's security force that ran the concentration camps. They were ultimately responsible for carrying out the Nazi plan to kill the Jews of Europe.) The terrible conditions at Bergen-Belsen, when the British had freed the camp in April, had shocked the world. (See p. 280.) Forty-five defendants, including twenty-one women, were charged. Fourteen were found not guilty. Eleven, including two women who had tortured prisoners, were sentenced to death and hanged. The rest received prison sentences.

The International Military Tribunal

But the people accused in these first trials had been directly involved in killings, either in mass shootings as at Krasnodov, or at camps like Majdanak and Bergen-Belsen. They were not leaders sitting far away in Berlin, Germany's capital. Although they were murderers, they were not the people who had decided on and planned the extermination of millions.

Perhaps even more important than punishing the guilty, the Allies—especially the United States—were determined to destroy the entire Nazi system. In the words of the high command of the American armed forces, "Nazism must be completely and finally removed from all aspects of German life." This not only meant barring active Nazis from official posts, but also removing their supporters from important positions in the economy, in the press and broadcasting, in the arts, and in education. "Nazi teachings and doctrines must be wiped out." The entire process was called "denazification."

Punishing war criminals was believed to be one of the ways to accomplish the denazification of Germany. The Allies decided to create a special international court, called the International Military Tribunal, to put the Nazi leaders on trial. The four countries that occupied Germany, the United States, Great Britain, the Soviet Union, and France, were represented. The

Denazification

At the same time as the war crimes trials, the Allied administrators of defeated Germany were making other efforts to wipe out the remains of Nazism. At the beginning of the Allied occupation, thousands of Germans were arrested and investigated by the Allied military authorities. In order to participate in public life, people were required to answer questions about their activities during the Nazi period. They were then classified as "major offenders," "offenders," "lesser offenders," "followers," or as non-Nazis. Depending on the category, the person might be arrested and tried, fined, or banned from certain activities such as holding public office.

The denazification process caused great resentment among many Germans. People who had played a minor part in the government during the Nazi years and told the truth were sometimes treated more harshly than those who had been fanatical Nazis but lied. In addition, the system worked differently in the four zones of Germany. The Americans tended to take it most seriously, but even the American authorities would overlook the Nazi past of someone who was important in building up the German economy or who could help them in the growing conflict with the Soviet Union. (The most famous example is of the German scientists who became very important in the American missile and space programs. During the war, these men had worked in the German rocket program, which depended heavily on the use of slave labor.) In all three western zones, many judges, lawyers, and police officials who had served throughout the Nazi period continued in office. In the Soviet zone, those former Nazis who cooperated with the new communist set-up were often allowed to retain positions of authority.

trial was held at Nuremberg in southern Germany, where the Nazi Party had held its rallies, and where the racial laws against the Jews had been proclaimed. (See Chapter 3, pp. 70–71.)

The charges

The defendants included twenty-two men and six organizations. The first set of charges against them was that they had committed "crimes against peace." Although going to war was not itself a crime, this charge indicated that a country was justified in going to war only to defend itself or another country. Basically, this meant the Nazis were charged with planning and waging wars of conquest. Some observers at the time, and some historians afterwards, have argued that the winners of any war might claim the same thing about their defeated enemies. The four countries that put the German leaders on trial could all be accused of having started a war to conquer territory sometime in their history.

The second set of charges involved "war crimes." These are acts that are against "the laws and customs" of war. Included in the definition were the use of civilian populations of conquered countries as slave workers, killing hostages, mistreating prisoners of war, and the complete or "wanton destruction of cities, towns, or villages" as well as "destruction not justified by military necessity." Many of these actions violated treaties that Germany had signed.

But the Nazi leaders were also charged with a third set of actions, described as "crimes against humanity." This was a new idea. These crimes included "murder, extermination, enslavement, deportation [forcibly removing people from their towns of residence], and other inhumane acts committed against any civilian population, before or during the war." They also included "persecution on political, racial or religious grounds ... whether or not in violation of the domestic [national] law of the country where perpetrated."

With these charges and definitions, the Allies were saying that the Nazis had done things that had to be considered crimes in all circumstances and at all times—even if the actions were considered "legal" by the government in power at that time. The idea of a "crime against humanity" meant that even if German law allowed the extermination of the Jews, it was still a crime to carry it out. In fact, even the Nazis never passed a law that openly allowed murder. But other forms of persecution of the Jews had been "legal" under the Nazis. They had passed laws to take away the jobs and property of Jews, to expel them from school, to force them to leave Germany. They had made it a crime for a Jew to marry a non-Jew. Later, in occupied Poland, they had issued decrees forcing Jews to move to the ghettos. Throughout Europe, they had ordered that Jews be deported from their homes. Now these actions would be judged as part of the "crimes against humanity" that led to mass murder.

Although the charges against the Nazi leaders did not single out the attempted destruction of the Jews, the trial that followed nevertheless often focused on the Holocaust.

The main Nuremberg trial

The rules of the International Military Tribunal that presided over the Nuremberg trials stated that "leaders" and "organizers" who participated in deciding or carrying out a plan to commit crimes against humanity were "responsible for all acts performed by any person in executing such plan." In other words, the men who planned the extermination of the Jews would be held responsible for the actual killings, even though these were carried out by others. High-level officials were still guilty, even if they themselves had never gone near a concentration camp.

The rules created for the tribunal also rejected the idea that "following orders" was an excuse. Even if a person had been ordered by his official superior to commit such an act, it was still a crime. So lower-level Nazis could not claim that they were not guilty because the plans had been made without their knowledge and they were just carrying them out. This was especially important because every Nazi was claiming that some higher Nazi had given him orders. If this argument had been accepted, it would have meant that only Hitler and perhaps a handful of others could have been held responsible.

The International Military Tribunal sat from November 18, 1945, until November 1, 1946. An extraordinary amount of evidence was presented by the prosecutors from each of the four countries. (A Justice of the United States Supreme Court, Robert Jackson, was the chief American prosecutor.) While most of the defendants denied their involvement in the Holocaust, or even their knowledge of it, none claimed that the events had not occurred. There were too many witnesses, including German officials such as the commandant (commander) of Auschwitz, Rudolph Höss. There were too many detailed documents that the Nazis had failed to destroy. Instead, the leaders of the Nazi regime claimed that the systematic attempt to destroy the Jewish people had not

been their own individual responsibility. It was the work of someone else's department, it was someone else who made the decisions, it was someone else who gave the orders.

The defendants

The following defendants at the main Nuremberg trial were found guilty, sentenced to death, and, except where noted, were hanged:

Martin Bormann was Hitler's deputy from 1941 to 1945. He was the only defendant not present at the trial, either having escaped or, more likely, having died in Berlin in 1945. He was sentenced to death but never found.

Hans Frank was one of Hitler's earliest supporters and his personal lawyer. During the war, he was governor-general of occupied Poland. (See Chapter 5, pp. 118–20.)

The defendants being tried before the International Military Tribunal in Nuremberg. Seated left to right: Hermann Göring, Rudolf Hess, Joachim von Ribbentrop, and Wilhelm Keitel.

Wilhelm Frick had helped the Nazis from their earliest days; he had been one of Hitler's co-defendants at his trial for treason in 1924. (See Chapter 2, pp. 30–31.) Eventually he became Minister of the Interior in the Nazi government, in charge of police forces, until he was replaced by Heinrich Himmler.

Hermann Göring was long the second most important Nazi, after Hitler himself. He was, among other things, the head of the air force and in charge of economic planning. He was famous for his vast collection of art, looted from all over occupied Europe. After the trial, he committed suicide with poison before he could be hanged.

Alfred Jodl was Chief of the General Staff of the Armed Forces. Although he claimed he was only a military man who carried out the orders of his superiors, Jodl ordered the shooting of hostages and was involved in planning anti-Jewish actions.

Ernst Kaltenbrunner became head of the Main Office for Reich Security, known as the RSHA (see box p. 181) in 1943, after the assassination of Reinhard Heydrich. The RSHA was the organization that was directly in charge of the Holocaust.

Wilhelm Keitel was Chief of the High Command of the Armed Forces. He issued the notorious Commissar Order, which ordered the army to shoot captured Soviet officials, including prisoners of war. (See Chapter 7, pp 184–85.) He signed the "Night and Fog" decree, under which captured resistance members in western Europe were made to disappear without a trace.

Joachim von Ribbentrop was Hitler's Foreign Minister from 1938 until the defeat of Germany. He pressured German allies and satellites to deport Jews to extermination camps.

Alfred Rosenberg had been the Nazis' leading "philosopher" of racism, and was considered one of their main "experts" on Jewish culture. From 1941 to 1943, he was in charge of a large section of captured Soviet territory, and was heavily involved in supervising the Final Solution (the extermination of the Jewish people) there.

Fritz Sauckel was an early Nazi who became head of Germany's Labor Department in 1942. This put him in charge of a vast program of slave workers from all over Europe forced to work in the war factories of Germany.

The front page of Der Stürmer, *the Nazi newspaper edited by Julius Streicher.*

Artur Seyss-Inquart was an Austrian Nazi who served as Governor-General Hans Frank's deputy in Poland and then was in charge of the occupied Netherlands, where his policies were exceptionally brutal. (See Chapter 10, pp. 297–98).

Julius Streicher was the founder and editor of the newspaper *Der Stürmer.* This newspaper stood out even among Nazi papers both for the viciousness of its attacks on Jews and for its semipornographic content. The long-time Nazi leader in Nuremberg, Streicher was responsible for storm trooper attacks against Jews and for the destruction of the Nuremberg Synagogue in 1938.

The following defendants were found guilty and sentenced to prison:

Karl Dönitz was commander of the German navy, and briefly the second Führer after Hitler's death. He was acquitted of "crimes against humanity" but sentenced to ten years in prison for "crimes against peace" and for war crimes.

Walther Funk played an important role in winning business support for the Nazis before they gained power. Later he was head of the Bank of Germany, where loot taken from the victims of the Holocaust, including gold teeth, was sent. Funk was sentenced to life in prison, but was released in 1957, when he was sixty-seven years old, because of ailing health.

Rudolf Hess was another very early Nazi, and was Hitler's deputy until 1941. At that time, in the middle of the war and without the knowledge of the other Nazi leaders, he flew a plane to Britain, apparently hoping to arrange an end to the war. Denounced by Hitler as crazy, he was held prisoner by the British for the rest of the war. He was not in Germany while the Holocaust was actually carried out. Hess was sentenced to life in prison and committed suicide there in 1987, at the age of 93.

Constantin Von Neurath was a diplomat who was Foreign Minister when Hitler took power. He retained that job in Hitler's government until replaced by Joachim von Ribbentrop in 1938. Later he was named "Reich Protector of Bohemia and Moravia" (today's Czech Republic), when Germany destroyed Czechoslovakia. But he was probably not tough enough for the Nazis and was replaced in that post by Reinhard Heydrich, one of the main architects of the Holocaust. Von Neurath was sentenced to fifteen years in prison, but was released after eight years, at the age of eighty-one.

Erich Raeder was commander of the German navy until replaced by Karl Dönitz in January 1943. He was sentenced to life in prison.

Baldur von Schirach had been head of the Hitler Youth (see Chapter 4, pp. 99–100), and later Nazi Party leader in Vienna, Austria. He was sentenced to twenty years imprisonment.

Albert Speer was Hitler's favorite architect and later Minister of Armaments and War Production, where he made extensive use of slave labor. Almost alone among the Nazi leaders, Speer expressed a sense of regret for his actions, although he maintained that he did not know about the extermination of the Jews. Speer was sentenced to twenty years in prison, which he served. The book he wrote after his

release, *Inside the Third Reich,* is an extremely valuable source of information.

The following defendants were found not guilty:

Hans Fritzsche was the head of German radio.

Franz von Papen was an old-line conservative politician who was Chancellor of Germany (head of the government) before Hitler, and helped Hitler come to power in 1933. (See Chapter 2, pp. 48–50.) He later served as a German ambassador.

Hjalmar Schacht was Hitler's Minister of Economics from 1934 to 1937. His policies were probably responsible for the improved economic conditions in Germany in those years. (See Chapter 4, pp. 100–02.) Schacht had connections with anti-Hitler plotters in the German government and army and was imprisoned by the Nazis near the end of the war.

Spandau Prison, in Berlin, Germany, where Albert Speer, Minister of Armaments and War Production, served his term and Rudolf Hess, Adolf Hitler's deputy until 1941, was imprisoned until his suicide in 1987.

Two other individuals were included in the original charges, but were not tried:

Robert Ley had been head of the Nazi "German Labor Front" that replaced the free trade unions. (See Chapter 2, p. 58.) He committed suicide before the trial.

Gustav Krupp von Bohlen was the head of the giant Krupp steel and armaments company that had used slave labor throughout the war. He was considered too ill and was never tried.

Organizations

Six organizations or groups were also defendants at the main Nuremberg trial. At the conclusion of the trial, four of the organizations were declared to be "criminal organizations." Individual members of these groups could be charged with crimes for participating in them. Two organizations, the General Staff and High Command of the German Armed Forces and the Reich Cabinet (the highest officials of the government), were found not guilty. The organizations that were found guilty were:

Gestapo (secret police)

Leadership Corps of the Nazi Party

Sturmabteilungen or SA (storm troopers or "brownshirts")

Schutzstaffel or SS (black-uniformed "security force" of the Nazi Party that ran the concentration camps) including the *Sicherheitsdienst,* or SD (security police)

The later Nuremberg trials

The first trial, of the top leaders of the German government, military, and Nazi Party, was followed by a series of twelve other Nuremberg trials. The defendants in each of these trials represented a different aspect of the way Nazi Germany had carried out its crimes. For example, the first trial was of doctors and other medical personnel. These were people who had participated in the "selection" process at extermination camps, engaged in medical experiments on prisoners, and had otherwise used their medical knowledge to commit crimes. The eleventh trial, the "Ministries Case," involved high officials of various departments of the German

government, some of whom were not Nazis, who had in various ways helped carry out the Nazi policy of mass murder. The twelfth trial, the "High Command Case," was of high military officials.

Together, the evidence presented at these twelve trials showed how every department of the German government, the military, and large sections of private industry were all involved in the crimes that the top Nazis had planned. In this sense, the Nuremberg trials were "show trials." This does not mean that the trials were not fair. A significant number of defendants were found not guilty. All had lawyers to defend them. All their legal rights were observed. But the purpose of the trials was not simply to punish individual criminals. It was also to educate the public, including the German public, about what had happened and how it had happened.

But as time passed, the political situation in Europe changed. The western Allies, the United States, Britain, and

The judges' bench at the Nuremberg trials. The United States, Britain, France, and the Soviet Union each had one voting judge and one alternate judge.

France, came into increasing conflict with the Soviet Union. Germany, the former enemy, was seen as an important partner in this conflict, which soon became known as the "Cold War." Trials of war criminals, and harsh punishments of those found guilty, were beginning to interfere with the goal of making Germany into a strong supporter of the west. Soon the conflict with the Soviet Union led to the creation of two separate Germanies. The Soviet Zone of occupation became East Germany (the German Democratic Republic), a Communist country dominated by the Soviet Union. The American, British, and French zones became West Germany (the Federal Republic of Germany), a strong ally of the west. Soon, West German political parties and churches were pressing for the end of war crime trials, and for the release of many of those who had been convicted. By the early 1950s, only a few years after the end of the war and the Holocaust, very few former Nazis remained in prison.

A summary of the twelve trials at Nuremberg

1. The Medical Case began on November 11, 1946 (less than two weeks after the judgment in the original Nuremberg trial of top Nazis), and ended on August 20, 1947. There were twenty-three defendants, of whom seven were found not guilty. Seven defendants were hanged, and five others received life imprisonment; all of these were eventually reduced to either fifteen or twenty years.

2. The Milch Case ran from November 13, 1946, to April 17, 1947. It had a single defendant, who was involved in the administration of the slave labor system. He was sentenced to life in prison, which was reduced to fifteen years, but was released in 1954.

3. The Justice Case, which ran from January 4 to December 4, 1947, involved people who had been part of the Nazi legal system, including judges in the special Nazi courts. There were sixteen defendants, though one committed suicide and one was not tried because of his health. Four defendants were found not guilty, the others received sentences ranging from five years to life, but all were released in 1950 and 1951.

4. The Pohl Case, from January 13 to November 3, 1947, included eighteen defendants who were involved in the eco-

During the Medical trial, a victim shows her scarred leg to the court while an expert witness explains the medical experiment performed on her.

nomic aspects of the Holocaust, including the administration of slave labor and running companies owned by the SS. Three were acquitted, and four were sentenced to death. Only one death sentence was carried out: the main defendant, Oswald Pohl, who was head of the Main Administrative Office of the SS, was hanged.

5. The Flick Case ran from February 8 to December 22, 1947. This was a trial of six people involved in the coal and steel industry. Three were found not guilty. The heaviest sentence was seven years, but all the prisoners were released by 1950.

6. The I. G. Farben Case was tried from May 8, 1947, to July 30, 1948. I. G. Farben was the giant German chemical company that had, among other things, built a plant at Auschwitz (known as Auschwitz III) to use slave labor. (See Chapter 9, pp. 273–74.) There were twenty-four defendants, one of whom did not stand trial because of poor health. Ten

The panel of judges at the I. G. Farben trial listen to testimony.

were found not guilty, and the others received prison sentences of up to eight years. After their prison terms, many of them resumed their highly successful business careers.

7. The Hostage Case involved German military personnel involved in executing hostages. It began on May 10, 1947, and ended on February 19, 1948. Of the twelve men charged, one committed suicide, one was too ill to stand trial, and two were found not guilty. The others received sentences ranging up to twenty years, but all were released by 1953.

8. The RuSHA Case ran from August 1, 1947, to March 10, 1948. The RuSHA was the "Race and Resettlement Main Office" of the SS. This organization was in charge of making sure that SS members were "racially pure" and was involved in the plans of Heinrich Himmler, the head of the SS, to make the SS into the model for the future German "super race." Of the fourteen defendants, one was found not guilty. A few were given sentences ranging up to twenty-five years, but

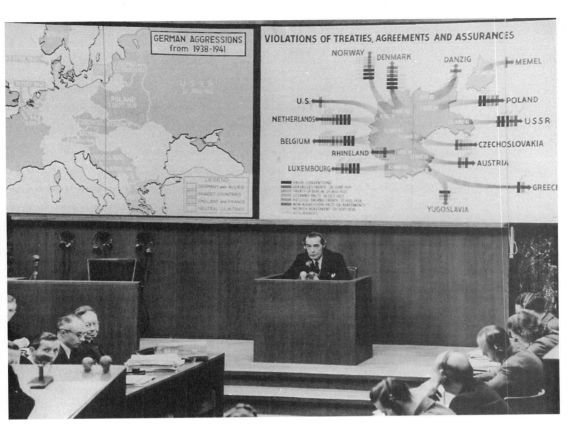

most were sentenced to the time they had already spent in prison before and during the trial.

9. The *Einsatzgruppe* Case began on July 3, 1947, and ended on April 10, 1948. The *Einstatzgruppen* were the specially trained units that carried out mass shootings during the invasion of the Soviet Union. (The formation and activities of the *Einsatzgruppen* are described in Chapter 7, pp. 192–93.) There were twenty-four defendants, one of whom committed suicide before the trial and one of whom died shortly after the trial. Fourteen were sentenced to death, although only four were executed. The others had their sentences reduced to prison terms. At this trial, the detailed testimony of Otto Ohlendorf, the commander of *Einsatzgruppe* D, included horrifying descriptions of mass executions, including of children. Ohlendorf was one of those hanged.

10. The Krupp Case was held from August 16, 1947, to July 31, 1948. The defendants were part of the management

Theodore Monbostel, former Foreign Minister of Austria before the Nazi occupation, testifies for the prosecution at the Ministries trial.

of the giant Krupp iron and steel company, which had used large numbers of slave workers during the war. The twelve defendants received sentences ranging from two to twelve years, but all were released by 1951.

11. The Ministries Case ran from November 14, 1947, to April 13, 1948. The twenty-one defendants were officials of various government departments such as the Foreign Ministry. Two were found not guilty, and the others received prison terms between three and twenty years. These longer terms were later reduced to ten years, and most of the other defendants were released in 1950 and 1951.

12. The High Command Case was tried from November 28, 1947, to October 28, 1948. Of the fourteen high-ranking military men charged, two were acquitted and two received life in prison. One of these sentences was reduced to eighteen years; the other defendant sentenced to life imprisonment was released in 1954, as were most of the other defendants in this trial.

Trials in other countries

The special Nuremberg court was created to try people for crimes that had not taken place in one particular place. The Allies agreed that most war criminals should be tried in the countries where their crimes had occurred. One country where the Nazi system of mass murder had been centered was Poland. Poland had been the home of the largest Jewish community in Europe, and three million Polish Jews had been killed. Another three million non-Jewish Poles had died at the hands of the Nazis. In addition, Poland was the location of the extermination camps to which Jews from the rest of Europe had been sent.

After the war, the Polish government established a special Supreme National Court to try especially important cases. One of these was the trial of Rudolf Höss, the first commandant of Auschwitz, along with other Auschwitz personnel. The evidence presented at this trial showed every detail of how Auschwitz was established and operated. Others convicted by the Polish Supreme National Court included Arthur Liebehenschel, who replaced Höss as Auschwitz commander; Ludwig Fischer, the German governor of Warsaw who set up the Treblinka death camp (see Chapter 8); and Amon Goeth, the brutal commander of the Plaszów concentration camp. With very few exceptions, those found guilty were sentenced to death and hanged.

In addition, other Polish courts also tried many war criminals. Among those convicted and executed were Hans Biebow, the German administrator of the Lódz ghetto (see Chapter 5, pp. 132–42), and SS General Jürgen Stroop, the commander of the forces that defeated the Warsaw ghetto uprising and destroyed the ghetto. (See Chapter 6, pp. 171–76.)

In many countries, the main targets of trials after the war were citizens of those countries who had helped the Germans during the occupation. This was especially true in the first months after the defeat of the Germans. Although the persecution and deportation of the Jews were among the accusations against these people, it was not the main focus. Instead, those who helped the Germans were thought of as traitors more than as war criminals. In France, for example, thousands of these "collaborators" were shot immediately after the liberation of the country. Their trials often paid little attention to legal formalities. (See Chapter 11.)

In the Netherlands, more than fourteen thousand people were convicted. Over one hundred were sentenced to death, although only thirty-nine of these were actually executed. By 1960, only fifteen years after the war, less than fifty people remained in prison, and all but four were released that year.

In Hungary, 19,000 people were convicted as war criminals. Many of them, including four former prime ministers, were hanged. Among them was Ferenc Szálasi, leader of the Nazi-like Arrow Cross Party, that had helped the Germans deport and kill 450,000 Hungarian Jews. (See Chapter 12.)

The West German courts tried over 90,000 people through 1985. However, relatively few were convicted, and most sentences were lenient. Approximately 6,500 people received "substantial sentences."

The Eichmann Trial

The most important trial after the main Nuremberg trial occurred in 1961. This was the trial of Adolf Eichmann. In 1960, he was found living under a false name in Argentina. Israeli agents secretly kidnapped him and brought him to

Sympathy in South America

Nazi Adolf Eichmann had been a prisoner of the U.S. Army at the end of World War II, but his real identity was not known. When he was released, he continued to live in Germany for another five years, using false papers. In 1950, he was able to move to Argentina, again using false papers, and was later joined by his family.

Eichmann was not the only wanted Nazi to live secretly in Germany and then escape to South America. Another was Josef Mengele, the chief doctor at Auschwitz who "selected" who should be gassed and who should live, and who performed ghastly medical "experiments" on twins and other prisoners, most of them children. (See Chapter 9, pp. 263–65.) Another was Klaus Barbie, discussed later in this chapter (p. 377).

The escape of Eichmann, Mengele, and others was made possible by a network of Nazi sympathizers in Germany and by pro-Nazi elements that had influence in some South American governments such as Paraguay and Argentina. This is probably the reason that Israeli agents kidnapped Eichmann from Argentina, rather than ask the Argentine authorities for his arrest.

Argentina protested the kidnapping, which was clearly an illegal act by Israel. At the United Nations, Israel formally apologized to Argentina, but was allowed to keep Eichmann in custody.

Israel. Members of the Israeli parliament have said that when they heard Prime Minister David Ben-Gurion announce that Eichmann had been captured and was now in Israel, they were swept by feelings of joy. Eichmann was the most wanted Nazi in the world.

In his early career as a Nazi, Eichmann was appointed by Reinhard Heydrich to force Jews to leave Austria and then Germany. (See Chapter 3, pp. 79–80.) Then Eichmann was head of the "Jewish Affairs Section" of the Main Office for Reich Security, or RSHA, the organization that directly ran the Holocaust. (See box on p. 181.) Eichmann was one of the organizers of the Wannsee conference, when officials of the German government were informed that the Nazis had decided on the "Final Solution" to the "Jewish problem"—the physical extermination of the Jews. (See Chapter 7, pp. 200–02.) He planned and supervised the deportation of millions of Jews from all over Europe. He personally directed the deportation of the Hungarian Jewish community to Auschwitz. (See Chapter 12, pp. 342–44.) More than any individual except Heinrich Himmler, the head of the SS, and the assassinated Reinhard Heydrich, Eichmann was most responsible for carrying out the "Final Solution."

History on trial

Now Eichmann was in Israel, the Jewish nation that had been established in Palestine in 1948 (see Chapter 3, pp. 84–86), charged with "crimes against the Jewish people." Unlike the defendants at Nuremberg who were charged with "crimes against humanity," Eichmann was specifically accused of attempting to destroy the Jews as a people. Like the Nuremberg trial, however, the Eichmann trial was intended to do more than punish one individual. The leaders of Israel wanted to remind the world of the crimes committed against the Jewish people in Europe. They wanted to educate their own people, especially the younger generation, about the complete destruction of Jewish communities that had seemed so permanent. The Israeli leaders believed that the establishment of Israel, and its protection, was the only way Jews could truly be safe.

Although there were many thousands of Holocaust survivors in Israel, most rarely spoke about it before the Eichmann trial. Many felt guilty that they had survived the Holocaust, when so many others, often including their entire families, had died. The fact that this feeling of guilt was not justified did not make it any less painful. Many survivors simply could not bear to describe the almost unbelievable suffering they had endured. The Eichmann trial focused the eyes of Israelis, and of people throughout the world, on these experiences, and allowed the survivors to begin to speak about their ordeal.

Eichmann was questioned by Israeli investigators for eleven months. His condition was checked by doctors twice a day. A guard tasted all his food, to make sure no one tried to poison him. Each day a word-for-word transcript of Eich-

Spectators in the main hall of the Eichmann trial, held from April to July 1961.

mann's statement was taken, and Eichmann checked it for accuracy the next day. These transcripts totaled 3,500 pages.

The trial

The trial itself lasted four months, beginning in April 1961. It was held in a theater that had been converted for the trial and held 750 spectators. Eichmann himself sat in a specially constructed bullet-proof booth. He was defended by a German lawyer who had represented defendants at Nuremberg. The lawyer's fee was paid by Israel.

The three judges who presided over the trial (Israel does not use juries) had all been born and educated in Germany, but had come to Palestine as young men, before the Holocaust. When they questioned Eichmann, they spoke German to him. When Eichmann testified in German, the judges could understand him without a translator.

The courtroom was jammed for each of its 114 sessions. The world press crowded into the courtroom. It was broadcast by Israeli radio and television, the first time in history that a trial was televised. People listened to the sessions on busses going to work, at home, even on the streets through loudspeakers. The trial was video-taped, again the first time this had ever been done.

Over a hundred witnesses testified, and almost fifteen hundred documents were presented. Many of the highly incriminating documents were signed by Eichmann himself. The entire history of Nazi policy towards the Jews, from the earliest days of the Nazi government, was brought out. Witnesses described what the Nazis had done in each country they had occupied. The prosecutors made sure that there was at least one witness from each country where the Nazis had attempted to carry out the Final Solution. The ghettos, deportations, concentration camps, and death camps were explained by survivors.

The emotions in the courtroom were very visible. One witness, who had warned the prosecutors that he did not think he would be able to relive these experiences, had a stroke while on the witness stand. Several times spectators began shouting and had to be removed from the courtroom by guards. Sometimes the prosecutors were so overcome by the answers of the witnessers that they were unable to ask their next questions.

"Why didn't you resist?"

One of the reasons that Holocaust survivors rarely spoke about their experiences before the Eichmann trial was a feeling that other people, especially native-born young Israelis, were ashamed of them. How could so many people have gone to their deaths without fighting back?

In fact, there had been a great deal of Jewish resistance. There were uprisings at Auschwitz (see pp. 274–76) and Treblinka (see p. 237), battles in the ghettos of Warsaw, Bialystok, Vilna, and many others (see Chapter 6), and important Jewish partisan (guerrilla) units in the Soviet Union, Poland, and France, among others.

But it is true that compared to the enormous losses they suffered, Jews were able to inflict only minor setbacks to the Nazis in military terms. Of course, the Jews of Europe had no government, no army, in many places no real organization at all. They were attacked by the might of a modern, technologically advanced country, its army, and its vast police forces. Usually, and especially at the beginning, the Jews could not know what was going to happen. The Nazis tried to deceive them in every way possible. And, perhaps most of all, the idea that the Nazis were trying to murder millions of people was almost impossible to accept. No one had any experience to compare it to.

The Israeli prosecutors asked witness after witness why they had not resisted. Perhaps, one of these witnesses later said, they wanted a clear statement that resistance had been almost impossible. But most of the witnesses had great difficulty describing the fear and helplessness they had felt at the time. How could anyone who was not there understand?

One answer came from Abba Kovner. Kovner had been commander of the United Partisan Organization in the Vilna ghetto and then had led Jewish partisans in the forests. In December 1941, Kovner had called on the Jews of Vilna to resist. "It is better to die fighting like free men than to live at the mercy of the murderers," he had said. So Kovner was not one of those who had gone "like sheep to the slaughter." He was a hero. But Kovner did not condemn the others. Instead, he tried to explain:

> There hovers a question in the air of this courtroom. 'Why did the people not revolt?' I, as a fighting Jew, resent this question.

> Only people with a strong will may do so. And people with strong wills are not to be found among the desperate and the broken.

> But even this war, which has been called a war of despair, created people who believed, people with faith that there was a cause to die for one hour earlier,

to sacrifice oneself for something that was greater than life.

Because of this despair in which people found themselves, where their image of humanity had been taken away from them, it was not easy to accept this call to action. This is not surprising, nor is it unusual.

On the contrary, it is a miracle that there existed a minority who believed in this call to action and did what they did during those years. The very existence of a fighting resistance—that was not rational. It was an amazing achievement.

Eichmann's defense: Following orders

Eichmann's defense was the only one he could realistically attempt. He did not deny any of the facts of the Holocaust. He did not deny his knowledge of these events. He admitted that his boss, Reinhard Heydrich told him: "The Führer [Hitler] has ordered the physical extermination of the Jews." He admitted that he had brought a message from Heydrich to the SS commander in Lublin, Poland, General Odilo Globocnik. "It ordered Globocnik to start liquidating a quarter of a million Polish Jews," Eichmann testified. He admitted that he had organized the transport trains that carried the Jews, a thousand at a time, to the gas chambers of Auschwitz.

As a defense, Eichmann claimed he was only a small cog in a giant machine. He said that he had been, for all practical purposes, only a clerk, or a messenger. Others made the decisions, and others carried them out. He only passed along the orders that were given to him. He had no decision-making authority. Yes, he had joined the Nazi Party knowing that it believed in the persecution of Jews. But, he said, if it had been up to him, he would have continued the policy of forcing Jews to leave Germany and Europe, not kill them. In a way, he said, he was a friend to the Jews, and especially to the Zionists, the people who were then trying to establish the Jewish state that became Israel. Just like the Zionists, he believed that Jews should leave Europe. And he had found that the Jews were happy to leave. But, asked the prosecutor, weren't the Jews happy to leave because of the fear they felt because of Nazi persecution? That was true, Eichmann admitted, but he was not responsible for creating that fear. Rather,

Eichmann in his bulletproof booth during his trial.

he claimed, he had been a man faced with a terrible situation and had done his best to make it better.

In fact, he was too soft-hearted for the job he had been given, he said. In Minsk in White Russia, he had watched a group of Jews being forced to jump into a pit and shot, he remembered: "I saw a woman hold a child of a year or two into the air, pleading." Eichmann claimed he was terribly upset by this scene, because he had children of his own.

Throughout his trial, and during his four weeks of testimony, Eichmann did his best to look and sound like a meek clerk, who had had no choice but to carry out the jobs he was given. He was no longer the SS colonel who had called himself a "bloodhound" who hunted down the Jews of Europe. He was no longer the cold-eyed killer who had offered to save a million Jews from extermination in exchange for ten thousand trucks, in a deal he had described as "goods for blood, blood for goods." (See Chapter 12, pp. 345–47.)

After several months of deliberations, the court announced its verdict on December 11, 1961. Eichmann was found guilty of all fifteen counts in the charges against him. The court explained that each time Eichmann had organized a train carrying a thousand Jews to Auschwitz, with full knowledge that they would be killed there, Eichmann was an accomplice in a thousand deliberate murders. Even, said the court, "if we had found that the accused acted out of blind obedience, as he himself argued, we would still have said that a man who took part in crimes of such magnitude, over several years, must pay the maximum penalty known to the law. This court sentences Adolf Eichmann to death."

The Israeli Supreme Court confirmed the verdict and sentence the following May, and the President of Israel denied Eichmann's appeal to commute (reduce) his sentence. Eichmann was hanged on June 1, 1962, the only time Israel has ever executed a criminal. Eichmann's ashes were scattered over the Mediterranean Sea.

Later trials

Trials of Nazi war criminals continued long after the war. Sometimes, new evidence against a particular individual appeared. Sometimes, Nazis who had been wanted for many years were finally found and arrested. One of these was Klaus Barbie, who had been head of the Gestapo in the French city of Lyons. Although wanted by the French, Barbie had worked as a secret agent for the American occupation authorities in Germany after the war. Later, probably with American help, he was able to disappear and then to move to the South American country of Bolivia. The French discovered his identity in 1972, but it took another eleven years before the Bolivian government sent him back to France for trial.

Barbie was known as the "Butcher of Lyons." Two of his many actions were particularly well known. He had orga-

Klaus Barbie, head of
the Gestapo in Lyons,
France, during his 1983
trial for war crimes.
Because new evidence—
or the criminals
themselves—surfaced,
trials of Nazi war
criminals continued long
after World War II.

nized a raid on a home for Jewish refugee children and had ordered the deaths of the forty-four children, all under the age of fourteen. And he had tortured to death Jean Moulin, an almost legendary hero of the French resistance. In 1983, Barbie was sentenced to life imprisonment. (France had abolished the death penalty.) He died in prison in 1990.

It was not until 1989 that a Frenchman was convicted of "crimes against humanity." This was Paul Touvier, head of the pro-Nazi Milice ("Militia") in Lyons, who worked closely with Barbie. Touvier, like Barbie, had twice been sentenced to death by French courts, but had not been captured. But unlike Barbie, Touvier was protected by French people, especially by elements within the French Catholic Church. Touvier was convicted of ordering the shooting of seven Jewish hostages in 1944, and sentenced to life in prison. He died in prison in 1996.

In October 1997, France began the trial of Maurice Papon. Unlike Touvier, who had been a Nazi-like thug, Papon had been an important official of the French government in the city of Bordeaux during the German occupation. (See Chapter 11.) From 1942 to 1944, among his other duties, he was in charge of handling "Jewish questions" in the Bordeaux region. After the war he had continued his public career and had been appointed to important offices. He was in charge of police and security in Paris for many years and was Budget Minister in the French government in the early 1980s. He therefore had powerful friends, and it took more than half a century after the defeat of the Germans to bring him to trial.

Papon was accused of working with the Germans to deport 1,560 Jews from Bordeaux to the French transit camp at Drancy. From Drancy, they were deported to Auschwitz. Papon denied that he knew that the Jews were being sent to their deaths. He claimed that he tried to protect them from the Germans. He even said that he "spent the occupation fighting for the Jews, and for others." In April 1998, Papon was convicted of helping the Germans illegally arrest and deport Jews, although the court found that he did not know that they were being sent to be killed. It sentenced him to ten years in prison, but Papon remained free while he appealed, a process that may take two years.

The Papon trial was only the second one of a Frenchman specifically for his role in the Holocaust, and the first of an important official. It will probably also be the last. Papon was eighty-seven years old when his trial began. Even someone who was a young man during the Holocaust would be close to eighty today. Anyone who was old enough to play an important part would be even older.

The witnesses who would testify, those who are still alive, would also be old people. The events they would be asked to describe happened when they were young, and it is becoming harder to rely on the accuracy of their memories.

John Demanjuk trial

The case of John Demanjuk illustrates these problems. He was a Ukrainian who moved to the United States after the war and became a U.S. citizen. Information was received that Demanjuk had been a guard at the Treblinka death camp known as "Ivan the Terrible." (Treblinka is discussed in Chapter 8, pp. 218–38.) After a lengthy process, Demanjuk

was found to have lied about his past when he entered the United States. He was stripped of his citizenship and sent to Israel for trial.

At his trial in 1986, survivors of Treblinka, now very old, identified him as the brutal guard. Documents seemed to support the identification. Demanjuk claimed that he had never been a guard at Treblinka, that the witnesses were mistaken, and that the supporting documents were forgeries.

Demanjuk was convicted and sentenced to death, the only person other than Eichmann to receive this sentence in Israel. But the sentence was not carried out. Instead, after a series of appeals and complicated examinations of the case in the United States, it became clear that there was not enough evidence to convict Demanjuk. There were too many lapses in the memories of the witnesses to be sure that they were right. No one today knows whether John Demanjuk was really the vicious "Ivan the Terrible" of Treblinka. Demanjuk was set free.

14

Remembering the Holocaust

I t has been more than half a century since the survivors in Nazi death camps were freed, and many of them—and the criminals who tried to murder them—have died or are old people today. But the Holocaust has not been forgotten. No one can forget the unprecedented evil of the carefully planned and organized attempt at genocide, the deliberate destruction of a group of people, by a powerful government. Recognizing that evil, and remembering it, has had a lasting effect on the way we view the world we live in. Since the Holocaust, laws and national and international policies have changed throughout the world, the new nation of Israel was formed, literature, music, and film reflect the imprint of the Holocaust on human memory and imagination, and museums display relics and representations of the past as they promote scholarship of the terrible event in the interest of a saner future.

The Germans and their past

Not surprisingly, one of the countries in which the Holocaust has had the most impact is Germany itself. When the new country of West Germany was created after World War II out of the American, British, and French occupation zones, its laws reflected a strong awareness of the Nazi past. The Nazi Party and Nazi flags, insignia, and uniforms were all banned by law in West Germany. Spreading hate against a particular religion or nationality, either in writing or in speeches, was made a crime. Another law made it a crime to deny the existence of the Holocaust. Although these laws mean that expressing certain opinions is illegal, the leaders of West Germany believed that some limits on free speech and press were necessary because of Germany's special history. There were also constitutional restrictions on the role of the German army, which was banned from serving outside its own borders.

Beginning in 1953, the West German government paid reparations, monetary payments totalling $58 billion, to victims of the Nazis. By doing this, West Germany acknowledged that the postwar German government bore responsibility for the acts that Adolf Hitler and the Nazis committed in the name of Germany. People were compensated for time they spent in confinement, for injuries and damaged health, and for loss of earnings in their professional lives. However, the West German government, and more recently the government of unified Germany, has refused to pay people for the slave labor they were forced to perform during the Nazi regime. At the same time, Germany has continued to pay pensions and other old-age benefits to those who worked in government jobs and who served in the army and police during the Nazi years, from 1933 to 1945.

The years of silence

While the German government accepted responsibility for the Holocaust, many Germans seemed to want to forget what had happened. During the years after the war, beginning in the early 1950s and continuing for a generation, most Germans did not want to talk about the Hitler years. The question of what individual Germans had done—or failed to do—was difficult to face. How many ordinary Germans had

supported Hitler? How many had done anything to oppose Nazi policies? How many ordinary soldiers had participated in rounding up Jews? Many Germans worked hard to make their lives better, to rebuild the German economy and the bombed-out cities. They succeeded in making West Germany one of the most prosperous countries in the world.

Most Germans denied that they had known about the extermination of the Jews. It is quite likely that most ordinary people did not know of the Final Solution,—the plan to exterminate the Jews of Europe—which the Nazis kept secret

A close-up of a damaged church in the center of Nuremberg, Germany. Its roof and tower were shattered by Allied bombing during World War II. After the war, many Germans worked hard to make West Germany one of the world's most prosperous countries.

as long as they could. But ordinary Germans certainly knew that Jews were being persecuted, fired from their jobs, their shops destroyed, their children expelled from German schools. They knew the Nazis beat Jews up on the street. They knew Jews were arrested simply for being Jews, and were forced to leave their country. They knew that the Nazi leaders blamed Jews for "forcing" Germany into war, and that they publicly threatened that the Jews would be destroyed for this. For more than a decade, Germans heard the leaders of their country call the Jews "sub-humans" and constantly compare them to dangerous germs that had to be wiped out.

Rather than deal with these issues, it was easier to try to forget about them. After the period of "denazification" and the first war crimes trials of the postwar years (see Chapter 13), silence about the Holocaust and the crimes that Germans had committed was the rule. Younger Germans did not know what their parents had done, did not know what questions to ask. But this period too came to an end. Perhaps it was simply that the next generation of Germans, who had been too young to play a part in the terrible events, wanted to know the truth about the history of their country.

The silence ends

In 1979, an American television miniseries titled *Holocaust* was broadcast in West Germany. This fictional drama followed the lives of an ordinary German Jewish family during the Nazi era, as well as the lives of non-Jews who came to support Hitler. When it was originally shown in the United States, it was generally well received, although many critics thought it was too much like a soap opera. But when it was shown in Germany, it had a tremendous impact. The whole country seemed to have watched it, and it instantly became the major topic of conversation for German people of all types. After its airing, the role of the German nation in the Holocaust was increasingly discussed and argued about by German historians and novelists, teachers and students, and political leaders.

In recent years, Richard von Weizäcker, the President of Germany, often spoke of Germany's shame and the need to remember the inhumanity of the country's Nazi past in order to prevent it from happening again. Von Weizäcker's many

Holocaust Denial

A few people, in Germany and elsewhere, deny that the Holocaust ever took place, or at least claim that the number of victims has been greatly exaggerated. They say that there is no evidence for the existence of gas chambers, that the Nazis never planned and never carried out the Final Solution.

It is difficult to treat these ideas as honest arguments. Hundreds of thousands of pages of documents captured at the end of the war confirm the facts. Photographs and movies exist. The evidence from thousands of witnesses is overwhelming. These witnesses include survivors, soldiers of the Allied armies who liberated the death camps and concentration camps, and the testimony of many Germans, including Nazis who described both the planning and the actual killing. The Nazi leaders tried at Nuremberg did not deny the facts that were presented or question the documents. Their defense was that they themselves were not responsible. The transcripts of these trials are available. Adolf Eichmann, at his trial in Israel, confirmed every basic fact; there are videotapes, as well as transcripts, of his testimony.

With all this evidence, how can anyone continue to doubt the history of the Holocaust? The answer is that, almost always, the people who deny the Holocaust are doing so because they accept the Nazis' ideas, especially their hatred of Jews. All the evidence, they think, has been invented by a vast conspiracy—a conspiracy run by the Jews. Like the Nazis, they think that Jews control the world.

The danger is that constant repetition of ideas like Holocaust denial will make them more acceptable, just as Nazi leader Adolf Hitler constantly repeated his "big lies" until they seemed believable. (See box on p. 47.) Especially with new means of communication, like the Internet, these lies reach many people who have no way of checking the source. The best defense against this is knowledge and education.

---

eloquent expressions of these ideas were made even more powerful by his own family history. His father, Ernst von Weizäcker, although never a Nazi, had been a high-ranking German diplomat under Hitler and was sentenced to five years in prison in the Ministries Case at the Nuremberg trials. (See Chapter 13, p. 368.) Since 1996, Germany has observed January 27, the anniversary of the liberation of Auschwitz, as the official Remembrance Day.

Hitler's willing executioners?

It is increasingly clear that younger Germans are no longer willing to forget about their country's past. Events that occurred after the 1996 publication of the American historian Daniel Goldhagen's book titled *Hitler's Willing Executioners* demonstrate the new desire of German youth to know what happened. The book is very controversial, arguing that ordinary Germans willingly took part in the Final Solution. Goldhagen argues they did this because—long before Hitler came to power—the country was dominated by an extreme form of anti-Jewish hatred. Goldhagen calls it "eliminationist anti-semitism."

Many other historians and scholars, both in Germany and elsewhere, strongly disagree with Goldhagen's argument. They do not believe Hitler succeeded simply because most Germans shared his extreme hatred of Jews, and they do not agree that the average German was completely willing—even eager—to participate directly in the mass murder of Jews because of this hatred.

After *Hitler's Willing Executioners* was attacked by other historians, Goldhagen visited Germany, defending his point of view in various cities. Everywhere he went, younger Germans filled the seats to hear him. Every auditorium was jammed. Although Goldhagen's opponents made many strong points, it soon became clear that the German audiences agreed with Goldhagen. Goldhagen's position—whether right or wrong, the most "anti-German" position possible—seems to attract deep interest from the young people of Germany.

Skinheads and neo-Nazis

In Germany through the 1990s, there have been vicious attacks against foreign-born people, especially Turkish people, living and working in Germany. "Skinheads" (members of youth gangs that are generally white-supremacists and are known by their close-shaven heads) and others have beaten foreigners and firebombed their homes. Some of these "neo-Nazis" ("new Nazis," people who accept or have revived Nazi ideas) use the stiff-armed "Heil Hitler" salute, wear swastikas (the Nazi Party symbol), and read Nazi literature. These incidents occurred with the most frequency in what was once the Communist East Germany during the period when it became part of a reunified Germany. The reunification of Germany in 1990 has caused many difficulties in eastern

Germany, including unemployment, which is especially high among young people.

Some observers believe that skinheads have deliberately chosen the Nazi insignia and language simply because they are the symbols of the most extreme rebellion possible in Germany today, and they want to show their dissatisfaction with the world in the strongest way they know. Other people are more alarmed, remembering that the Nazi Party was also once a tiny group that most people did not take seriously.

Israel and the Holocaust

The country of Israel was founded in 1948 by the Jewish community in Palestine. It fulfilled the dream of the political movement called Zionism of creating a modern Jewish country in the ancestral homeland of the Jewish people. Zionists had argued throughout the twentieth century that Jews could never really become part of the countries in which they lived, that they needed their own homeland, controlled by themselves, in order to be safe and free.

Until World War II (1939–45), Zionism was still a minority view among Jews. Many European Jews believed that they could successfully become part of the nations of Europe, that prejudice against Jews was growing weaker, and that in time Jews would be treated like anyone else. Most Dutch Jews, or French Jews, or German Jews, thought of themselves as Dutch or French or German people who happened to have a different religion. For these people, "assimilation" (blending in) was the answer, not Zionism.

In the great Jewish communities of eastern Europe, many Jews believed that the future of the Jews would be assured by the creation of a new society in which all people were treated equally, regardless of their ethnic background. Thousands of Jews joined the Bund, the General Jewish Workers Union, and other socialist organizations. They believed that workers, both Jewish and non-Jewish, would unite to create this new society and that religion would disappear as people became more enlightened. For these Jews, socialism was the answer.

Many others in eastern Europe rejected assimilation, antireligious socialism, and Zionism, too. These were the reli-

gious Jews, who wanted to lead lives centered on their own religion, in their own communities, following Jewish tradition and studying Jewish law. The return of the Jewish people to Zion, to Israel, which their religion told them that God had promised to the Jews, could only happen when the Jews were worthy and God brought them there. The safety and well-being of the Jews, they believed, depended on obeying God, not on political movements.

The Holocaust and Zionism

Before World War II, the European Jewish community consisted of many political and interest groups. The Holocaust changed the way they looked at their place in the world. In 1945, the shattered remnants of the Jews of Europe emerged from hiding, from the forests, from the concentration camps, and looked for a place to rebuild their lives. Many, especially those in western Europe, went home. But hundreds of thousands could not return. There was nothing

to go home to. Everyone had been killed or deported, every synagogue burned down. The local population remained hostile to them. Their homes, if they were still standing, had been taken over by others. In July 1946, a violent anti-Jewish riot in Poland killed forty-two people (see p. 396.)

Many of these Jews, a quarter million of them, now lived in "displaced persons" camps—sometimes in the same places where the Nazis had imprisoned them in concentration camps. To these people, and to many others, the goal of the Zionists—of a Jewish nation run by Jews, for Jews—seemed their only hope.

A child lights a Hanukkah menorah during a 1945 holiday celebration in the Zeilsheim displaced persons camp in Germany. Hanukkah comemorates the rededication of the Temple of Jerusalem in 165 B.C..

The creation of Israel

Perhaps Israel would have been created if there had been no Holocaust, but it clearly became much more attractive and urgent following the Holocaust. The suffering of the Jews had a powerful effect on people all over the world. Public opinion in many countries was much more favorable to supporting the establishment of Israel than it would have been otherwise. Non-Jews in America and much of Europe supported the creation of Israel as a home for the survivors of the Holocaust. For many Jews, including many who had not been Zionists before, a Jewish nation was the only way of insuring that Jews would never be the victims of another Holocaust.

In some ways, the whole history of Israel has been shaped by the experience of the Holocaust. Many Israelis see their country as creating a new kind of Jew, people who would never allow themselves to be victims without fighting back. Especially after the trial of Adolf Eichmann in Israel in 1961 (see Chapter 13, pp. 369–77), the history of what happened to the Jewish people of Europe has become a major part of Israeli life. Each year, on the anniversary of the Warsaw ghetto uprising (see Chapter 6, pp. 171–76), Israel observes Holocaust Remembrance Day. The entire nation stops everything for a minute of silence, announced by sirens. Public ceremonies are held to remember the victims and to remember the resistance. In every classroom, schoolchildren discuss the meaning of the Holocaust. At Yad Vashem, the Holocaust memorial in Jerusalem, a solemn ceremony is held.

France: Responsibility and apologies

For many of the countries of Europe, the experience of the Nazi occupation and their role in the Holocaust continue to haunt them. In France, it was not until 1995 that President Jacques Chirac acknowledged responsibility for French actions during the Holocaust. Until then, France had always maintained that the French government that had cooperated with the Nazi occupiers of their country did not represent France. The "real France," they said, had nothing to apologize for because it was represented by the Resistance and by those who continued to fight the Germans from outside France. (See Chapter 11.)

It wasn't until 1989 that a Frenchman, Paul Touvier, was tried specifically for his role in helping the Germans kill Jews. Not until 1997 was an official of the French government during the war, Maurice Papon, brought to trial on similar

charges, found guilty, and sentenced to ten years in prison. (See Chapter 13, p. 379.)

In 1997, shortly before Papon's trial began, the largest union representing the French police issued an apology for the important part the police had played in rounding up Jews throughout France on behalf of the Nazis.

The role of the Catholic Church during the Holocaust has been a subject of great controversy in France. Some Catholic priests and bishops publicly opposed the attacks on the Jews. Archbishop Jules-Gérard Saliège of the city of

Toulouse told Catholics that the "Jews are our brothers. No Christian dare forget that." Priests, nuns, and monks hid and protected Jews, especially the children of parents who had been deported, at great risk to themselves. The leader of the French church, Cardinal Pierre Gerlier, urged Catholics to refuse to give up these children to the Germans. For many years, these were the things that supporters of the church emphasized. But it was only a part of the truth.

In September 1997, an extraordinary ceremony was held at Drancy, the Paris suburb that had been the main transit point for Jews deported from France to Auschwitz. There, the French church publicly recognized its failures during the Holocaust. It apologized for the "constantly repeated anti-Jewish stereotypes" that it had spread, acknowledging that these stereotypes were, at least indirectly, a primary factor "in the historical process that led to the Holocaust."

Most of all, the Catholic Church apologized for its silence, especially its failure to protest the anti-Jewish laws passed by the French government during the war. "In the face of the persecution of Jews ... silence was the rule, and words in favor of victims the exception," the statement said. "The vast majority of church officials" went along with the government's policies. They "did not realize that they had considerable power and influence." Protests from the French church might have set off many other protests, the statement said. This public opposition could have helped create "a barrier" against the Holocaust.

"Today we confess that silence was a wrong. We beg for the pardon of God and ask the Jewish people to hear our words of repentance."

Switzerland: Banks, gold, and the Holocaust

Switzerland, which borders Germany, remained neutral through World War II, staying out of the war. Although Switzerland was a country that traditionally protected refugees escaping persecution in other countries, its record in regard to Jews fleeing the Nazis was very mixed. Switzerland was a place where many European Jews, especially German and Austrian Jews, opened bank accounts to try to protect their money from the Nazi authorities. Not all of the people depositing money in Swiss banks had a lot of money, but with the Nazis coming to power, many Jews felt safer with their money there.

Because Switzerland was traditionally neutral, people felt confident that their money would be available even if their own country was at war. Switzerland was also a stable country; political turmoil that might threaten the banks was very unlikely, which was a serious concern in the first half of the twentieth century. Swiss bankers had a reputation for honesty. And Swiss law allowed foreigners to have secret bank accounts, often identified only by a number. This meant it would be very difficult for the Nazis to trace this money and try to seize it.

After the war, many Jewish people who had Swiss bank accounts were dead. Their financial records had often been destroyed. But others had escaped to places like the United States or had survived the Holocaust and remained in Europe. In many other cases, the families of the victims were still alive. When these people tried to get information concerning Swiss bank accounts that they or their relatives had opened, the Swiss banks and the Swiss government put many obstacles in their path. For years, the Swiss claimed that they had found, and returned, all the accounts held by Holocaust victims.

The disputes continued into the 1990s. After a great deal of publicity and worldwide outcry, the banks began a new search of their records. Thousands of unclaimed foreign accounts dating to the Nazi period were found. The Swiss published lists of the names on these accounts and the towns where the depositors lived when the accounts were opened. These lists appeared in several newspapers throughout the world in 1997.

Although the Swiss said that most of these accounts were quite small and many were clearly unrelated to the Holocaust, Switzerland was heavily criticized for being "unable" to find these accounts for decades and for making no effort to contact the people involved. In fact, some newspaper reporters were able to find some of these people, or their relatives, by using the lists Switzerland published and looking them up in a phone book. The banks were supposed to have searched for these account-holders immediately after the war.

Stolen Nazi gold deposited into Swiss accounts during the war has also become an embarrassment to Switzerland. From 1933 to 1945, it is estimated that the Nazi government stole at least $8.5 billion worth of gold from the central banks of the countries Germany conquered during the war. This gold was the property of those countries, held in their central banks to back up the country's paper money. This gold is called "monetary gold," and it is well known that Nazi Germany deposited most of it in Swiss banks during the war. Sometimes the gold bars were still stamped with the name of the foreign country from which they had been taken, so the Swiss knew—or should have known—that the gold was stolen. Part—but only part—of this gold was returned by the Swiss banks immediately after the war.

The Nazis also looted "private gold"—gold that belonged to private businesses or individuals. (It was common for Europeans to try to keep some of their assets in gold, including jewelry, because they were afraid that paper money could lose its value in times of turmoil.) Of the $8.5 billion worth of stolen gold, almost one-third is now believed to have been private gold. Much of this was taken from Jews. A 1997 study by the World Jewish Congress estimated that 85 percent of this private gold ended up in Swiss banks.

Some of the private gold was gold coins or gold bars held by businesses. Some was jewelry, including wedding rings, that the Nazis took away from arrested or deported Jews. And some was the melted-down gold fillings taken from the teeth of the dead at Auschwitz and the other death camps. (See Chapter 8, pp. 232–33 and Chapter 9, pp. 256–59.) Some of the gold bars stamped with the Nazi swastika that lay in the vaults of the banks of Switzerland for fifty years were the last physical traces of murdered Jews.

Poland: Antisemitism without Jews

In Poland, where Jews were almost one-tenth of the population before the war, the almost complete destruction of the Jewish community drastically changed Polish cultural and artistic life. The population of the Polish capital, Warsaw, had been almost one-third Jewish. Yiddish, the everyday language of Poland's Jews, had been heard on its streets for as long as anyone could remember. Yiddish theater, Jewish

A Warsaw street with Jewish shops before Germany's invasion of Poland in 1939. Warsaw and the other Polish cities were the center of Jewish life in Europe before World War II.

shops and restaurants, community and cultural institutions, political parties, and religious schools—all had made Warsaw and the other cities of Poland the center of Jewish life in Europe.

At the end of the war, there were only 200,000 Jews left in the country, out of 3,300,000 before the German invasion. The Poles had cooperated less with the Nazis than any other occupied nation of Europe, but this did not mean they had been friendly to the Jews. While many Jewish lives were saved by the bravery of their non-Jewish neighbors, other Poles informed the Germans where Jews were hiding. There was a long tradition of antisemitism in Poland, and it did not disappear when the Nazis occupied the country or with the Holocaust. Antisemitism did not even disappear from Poland when the Jews did.

In July 1946, more than a year after the surrender of Germany, a Polish mob attacked Jews in the town of Kielce. It was a pogrom, an anti-Jewish riot or massacre, like those that had happened so often in eastern Europe. The Jews of Kielce had recently returned from Soviet territory, where they had escaped during the war. (The Jews who had remained in the town had all been killed by the Nazis.) The pogrom killed forty-two people, including children. A rumor had been spread that Jews had kidnapped Christian children to use their blood in Jewish rituals. These were the same false accusations, known as the "blood libel," that had been made against Jews since the Middle Ages (500–1450). Recent investigations have indicated that the pogrom may have been deliberately stirred up as part of complicated rivalries among Polish political groups.

The Kielce pogrom had a devastating effect on the remaining and returning Polish Jews. The "blood libel," a story it seemed no reasonable person in the twentieth century could believe, had been enough to send a mob on a murderous rampage. This had happened *after* the terrible suffering of the Jews during the Holocaust was known to everyone. Many Jews decided there was no place for them in Poland. One hundred thousand Jews left the country, many for Palestine, others for the United States.

In the next four decades, the remaining Jews of Poland continued to face periodic antisemitic campaigns. These campaigns were started by different factions of the new Communist government for their own purposes. Although there were no more pogroms, Jews were accused of disloyalty to Poland and forced out of jobs. More and more Jews left the country, and many of those who remained abandoned their Jewish identity and hid their Jewish origins. There were few Jews left in Poland, but—amazingly—there was still antisemitism. Even after the end of communism, political candidates of Jewish background were attacked for not being truly Polish.

As the twentieth century neared its end, the people of Poland seemed to come to terms with the story of Jewish life in Poland, a story that was an important part of the Polish nation for many centuries. There has been in Poland a revival of interest in Jewish history, but the Jews, with few exceptions, are not there to see it.

Other echoes

The Holocaust has led to an awareness that anti-semitism and other forms of racism can lead to the most ter-

A group of children survivors from the Bergen-Belsen concentration camp arrive in Tel Aviv, Israel in 1948. After the Holocaust, many Jews believed the only way to prevent another Holocaust was to establish a Jewish nation.

rible results. Many countries and institutions that were not directly involved in the Holocaust have been forced to rethink the way they have dealt with the Jews throughout history. Five hundred years after Spain expelled its Jews in 1492, the Spanish government acknowledged the wrongfulness of this action. The Catholic Church has, over the past thirty years, removed from its rituals and prayers the anti-Jewish language that helped create Christian intolerance of Jews. Pope John Paul II, who lived through the Nazi era as a young man secretly studying to become a priest in Poland, has spoken often of the Holocaust.

In March 1998, after eleven years of preparation, the Catholic Church issued a fourteen-page document titled "We Remember: A Reflection on the Shoah." ("Shoah" is the Hebrew word used to describe the Holocaust.) The document's main author, Cardinal Edward Idris Cassidy, described it as "more than an apology. This is an act of repentance." Through the document the Church states that many Christians failed to do enough to save Jews during the Holocaust, and it condemns all forms of antisemitism and anti-Jewish thought.

However, the Church's statement does not go nearly as far as many Jews would have liked, nor as far as the statement of the French church issued a few months earlier. The new document does not say that the Church, as an institution, had any responsibility for the Holocaust. It praises the German Catholic clergymen who condemned Nazism, but it does not mention that the Church signed an agreement with Hitler's government soon after he came to power. (The role played by the Catholic Church in the early years of the Nazi government is discussed in Chapter 4, pp. 97–98.) It points out that Jewish leaders thanked Pope Pius XII, who headed the Church beginning in 1939, for helping to save lives. But it never mentions the criticisms made of the pope for his failure to publicly condemn the Nazi persecutions of the Jews.

The Church admits in "We Remember" that many Christians held anti-Jewish prejudices based on religion. But it also states that the antisemitism of the Nazis, which was based on racial theories, "had its roots outside of Christianity," and that this racial—not religious—antisemitism was the basis of the Holocaust. In it the Church asks the question:

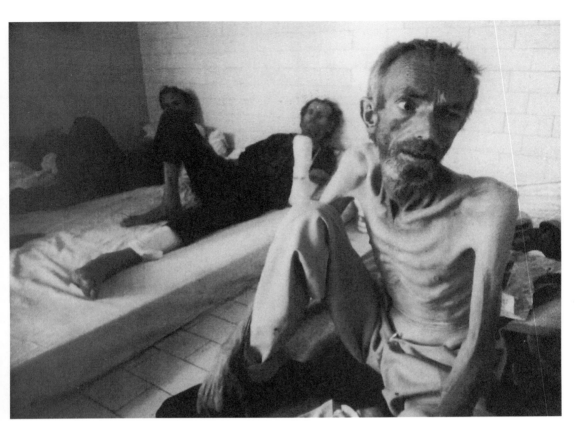

"Did anti-Jewish sentiments among Christians make them less sensitive, or even indifferent, to the persecution launched against the Jews" when the Nazis came to power? But then the Church notes that this question cannot be answered except on a case-by-case basis, because every person's thinking is shaped by many different influences.

Despite the importance of the issues left out of the document, many people view it as a significant step by the Church. The statement is intended to be used as a teaching document in Catholic universities, as well as seminaries where priests are trained. One part of the message is absolutely clear: "The Catholic Church therefore repudiates every persecution against a people or human group anywhere, at any time. She absolutely condemns all forms of genocide, as well as the racist ideologies that give rise to them."

In the 1990s, many people thought of the Holocaust when they learned of the "ethnic cleansing" that occurred

Bosnians in Serb internment camp in the mid-1990s. The ethnic cleansing that occured during the war in the former Yugoslavia in the 1990s recalls the genocide of the Holocaust fifty years earlier.

during the fighting among the different countries that had been part of Yugoslavia, including Serbia, Croatia, and Bosnia. Ethnic cleansing is the process by which one ethnic group, such as the Serbs, try to drive out members of other groups, such as Croats or Bosnian Muslims, from territory where both groups live. Ethnic cleansing means terrorizing people to force them to leave. It includes mass shootings of unarmed civilians, seizing all the men in a town and placing them in guarded camps where they are malnourished or even starved, exposed to the cold, and sometimes tortured. It includes systematic rapes of women and girls, intended to humiliate people as much as possible.

Perhaps because the public saw a resemblance to the Holocaust in the violence in Bosnia, pressure was placed on the countries of Europe and the United States to send troops to stop the murders. And although it has had little success so far, an international war crimes tribunal, modeled on the Nuremberg trials, has been created to try war criminals from the former Yugoslavia. Similarly, a war crimes tribunal was set up after the mass murders of one ethnic group by another during the 1990s in the east African nation of Rwanda.

Arts and the Holocaust

Just as lawmakers, politicians, historians, and philosophers have all struggled with the legacy of the Holocaust, writers, artists, composers, and filmmakers have worked to understand or represent the horrors, sacrifices, and heroism of the Holocaust through their art. In addition, museums and memorials in many countries exhibit representations and relics of the Holocaust.

Literature on the Holocaust

Noted writer Elie Wiesel was in Auschwitz and Buchenwald as a teenager. His first novel, *Night,* describes his own experiences. Wiesel's attempt to find meaning in the suffering of the Holocaust has made him an eloquent fighter against human rights abuses all over the world. He was awarded the Nobel Peace Prize in 1986.

The Italian Jewish writer Primo Levi was also in Auschwitz (see box on p. 278), and was one of those still in the camp when it was freed by Soviet soldiers, an event he later movingly described. Although he was a chemist before the war, Levi became a writer who returned to the theme of the Holocaust, and especially of Auschwitz, for the rest of his life. His first book, *If This Is a Man,* was published in 1947 and is subtitled *Survival in Auschwitz.* It is generally considered one of the finest works written on the Holocaust. Almost forty years later, he used the experience of Auschwitz as a way to explore the meaning of human life in *The Drowned and the Saved.* Levi's work is never sentimental or easy. He was able to describe the horrors he had seen in straightforward language that was extremely effective. Levi died at the age of sixty-eight in 1987.

It would be almost impossible for any Polish author to write a novel in the first twenty-five years after the war that did not reflect the author's thoughts and experiences of life during the German occupation of Poland. But few of the many Polish works reflecting the Polish war experience are well known to Americans. One exception is Jerzy Kosinski's 1966 novel *The Painted Bird,* a terrifying story possibly based on the author's own childhood experiences.

Elie Wiesel, Auschwitz survivor and author of Night, *was awarded the Nobel Peace Prize in 1986 for his fight against human rights abuses.*

Notable among German works on the Holocaust are two plays. Rolf Hochuth's 1964 play, *The Deputy,* strongly attacked the role of Pope Pius XII in failing to condemn Nazi antisemitism. Two years later, Peter Weiss published the play *The Investigation* which is closely based on the actual German trial of Auschwitz personnel.

German novelist Günter Grass wrote a well-known novel depicting the war years in Germany called *The Tin Drum* (1965). This is a funny and horrifying story about a child, Oskar, who purposely refuses to grow and wanders through Nazi Germany as a dwarf, playing his toy drum. Oskar's adventures brilliantly and mockingly capture the unbelievable reality of Nazism. A film version, directed by Volker Schlondorff, was released in 1979.

German poet Nelly Sachs, who fled from the Nazis to Sweden in 1940, won the Nobel Prize in 1996 for literature for her collection of poems *O the Chimneys*. Until her death in 1970, Sachs dedicated her career to giving a voice to those vicitms of the Holocaust.

American writer John Hershy's novel *The Wall* became a best-seller when it was published in 1950. It describes the daily life of the Jews in the Warsaw ghetto. (See Chapter 6.) Another American novel that was set in the Warsaw ghetto and became a best-seller was Leon Uris' *Mila 18*, published in 1960. Taking its title from the address of the secret headquarters of the Jewish Fighting Organization at number 18 Mila Street, the novel tells the story of the Warsaw ghetto uprising. Through these novels, American readers learned about both Nazi oppression and Jewish resistance.

Films on the Holocaust

Like literature, films have played an important role in bringing the subject of the Holocaust to the attention of millions of younger people.

Schindler's List

Perhaps no work about the Holocaust has had a greater effect than Steven Spielberg's highly successful 1994 film *Schindler's List,* which won many awards, including the Oscar as best picture. Filmed in black and white, it tells the fact-based story of Oskar Schindler, a German businessman with some shady practices, including connections with the Nazis. Mainly, Schindler was interested in making money.

In 1939, the Nazis put Schindler in charge of two Polish factories they had taken from Jewish owners. At first, Schindler welcomed this as an opportunity to get rich. However, in 1943 he witnessed the brutal deportations of Jews from the ghetto of Kraków (Cracow), the third largest city in Poland. Most of these people, including children, were sent to the Belzec death camp where they were murdered as soon as they arrived. (See Chapter 8). Some, however, remained near Kraków in the Plaszów labor camp, which was commanded by the evil SS Captain Amon Goeth. (The SS was an abbreviation for the *Schutzstaffel*, the "defense unit" of the Nazi Party.) Schindler, who saw what was happening, used

his friendship with Goeth to try to save Jews. (After the war Goeth was tried by the Polish Supreme National Court and hanged; see Chapter 13, p. 368.)

When the Soviet army began to drive the Germans out of Poland, Schindler moved his factory far to the west, in what had been Czechoslovakia. What was remarkable was that he insisted on taking his Jewish workers with him. Schindler and his workers knew that anyone left behind would be killed by the Nazis. So whether the name of a particular Jew was on the list of Schindler's workers meant life or death. This is the "Schindler's list" of the title. Incredibly, Schindler was even able to get three hundred women back from Auschwitz.

By the end of the war, Schindler was a different person. The movie shows him willing to sacrifice everything to save more people. Instead of thinking of himself as a hero for saving over one thousand Jews from certain death, Schindler feels guilty that he did not do more.

Oskar Schindler (second from right) poses with a group of Jews he rescued.

Anne Frank hid with her family for 25 months at the back of her father's store before they were found out by the Nazis.

Schindler died in 1974, and was buried in Jerusalem. The movie ends by showing survivors among "Schindler's Jews," along with their children and grandchildren, placing stones on his grave, in the Jewish tradition.

The Diary of Anne Frank

Sometimes, the presentation of a work of art about the Holocaust has changed to reflect different ideas that have evolved. One example is of the stage production of *The Diary of Anne Frank*. (The story of Anne Frank and the diary she wrote while hiding from the Nazis in Amsterdam is described in Chapter 10, pp. 307–09.) When *The Diary of Anne Frank* was first made into a Broadway play in 1955, it was extremely successful, winning the Pulitzer Prize for drama. A film, released four years later, was similar to the play.

Over the years, however, the play and movie were criticized. Some people felt that some of Frank's words had been taken out of context. The writers and producers of the Broadway play wanted to make Frank into a symbol of all of humanity. Because of this desire, it was argued, they played down Frank's Jewish identity. The specific nature of the Holocaust, that it was an attempt to destroy the Jews, was made to seem less important, these critics said, in order to make Frank's story more appealing to everyone. In addition, they argued, the play made Frank into a much more optimistic and hopeful person than she really was. This optimism, the critics said, improperly softened the terrible horror of what happened to Frank, to her family, and to the Jews of Europe.

In 1997, a new production of *The Diary of Anne Frank* opened on Broadway. Like the first version, it was based on the words Frank actually wrote in her diary. But the new play seemed to put more emphasis on Frank's anger and despair at what was happening to her.

Someone who reads Frank's diary for himself or herself can see that both the hopeful and despairing sides of Frank are part of her personality. They can also see that she never forgot that she was being hunted because she was Jewish, and that she came to think of her fate as tied to the fate of the Jewish people. At the same time, Frank thought of herself as Dutch, loved the country and its language, and wanted to be a Dutch writer.

Documentaries

Some of the most effective films that deal with the Nazi period have been documentaries (nonfiction films). *Night and Fog,* an early example, was made by the French director Alain Resnais in 1955 and deals specifically with concentration camps. Its title comes from the German order of 1941 ("*Nacht und Nebel*" in German) under which captured resistance fighters from western Europe were made to disappear without a trace, into night and fog. The film uses the phrase as a symbol of what the Nazis were trying to do, and the need to remember and take responsibility. Part of the film's impact comes from its contrasting use of black and white pictures taken when the concentration camps were liberated and color film of the camps taken years later when they were abandoned.

The French filmmaker Marcel Ophuls has made two major documentaries about the Holocaust. *The Sorrow and the Pity* (1970), which runs over four hours, includes many interviews with French people remembering the years of the German occupation. The film was a sensation in France because it emphasized that many French people had cooperated with the Nazis, and that many more simply "went along." (See Chapter 11.) Ophuls's *Hotel Terminus* (1987) tells the story of Klaus Barbie, the *Geheime Staatspolizei,* or the Gestapo, chief in Lyons during the occupation. (See Chapter 13, pp. 377–78.) The film won an Oscar as best documentary.

Another French documentary filmmaker is Claude Lanzmann. His *Shoah* is nine hours long. ("Shoah," which means a whirlwind of destruction, is the Hebrew word used for the Holocaust.) It uses interviews with witnesses, like the men who worked on the deportation trains or in the death camps or minor Nazi officials, shot especially for the film to explain the Holocaust. No pictures of the actual events are used. Slowly, detail after detail, the entire story of the Holocaust is revealed. More remarkable, many of Lanzmann's subjects reveal their own psychology, the hatreds and jealousies and prejudices that allowed the Holocaust to happen.

Other films

The number of fictional films that touch on Holocaust themes is very large. American films include *Judgment at Nuremberg* (1961), directed by Stanley Kramer, about one of the "lesser" Nuremberg trials. It includes memorable performances by major Hollywood stars including Spencer Tracey and Montgomery Clift. Clift, along with Marlon Brando and Dean Martin, is also one of the stars of *The Young Lions* (1958), directed by Edward Dmytryk, based on Irwin Shaw's novel. Brando plays a "decent" German who becomes an officer in Hitler's army; Clift's character is Jewish and he and Martin are American soldiers whose paths cross Brando's at the end of the war.

A more recent American film is *Sophie's Choice* (1982), directed by Alan J. Pakula and based on William Styron's novel of the same name. The film is about a young Polish woman in New York after the war whose memories of what she endured in Europe destroy her. Meryl Streep's portrayal of the title role won an Oscar.

The Damned (1969) is an Italian-West German film directed by the Italian Luchino Visconti. It tells the story of a powerful German family that becomes more and more enmeshed in Nazism.

The great Italian film director Vittorio De Sica made *The Garden of the Finzi-Continis* in 1970, which won an Oscar as best foreign film. It tells the story of a wealthy and cultured Italian Jewish family that tries to ignore the ever-increasing dangers in Nazi-dominated Europe.

The French director Louis Malle made two films set in German-occupied France. In *Lacombe, Lucien* (1974), he tells the story of a young Frenchman who, unable to join the resistance, instead joins the pro-Nazi Milice (see Chapter 11, p. 329), but then falls in love with a Jewish woman. *Au Revoir les Enfants* ("Goodbye, Children"; 1987), is one of Malle's last films. This is a beautifully told but heartwrenching story of a Jewish child hidden in a Catholic school who is eventually arrested and deported.

Memorials and museums

Yad Vashem

Yad Vashem, the memorial located on Remembrance Hill in Jerusalem in Israel, is both a museum of the Holocaust and an institution for its study. Yad Vashem has sponsored research and published many books on different aspects of the Jewish experience in Europe. It has also recorded the oral histories of many thousands of Holocaust survivors. As the survivors grow old and die, these records will continue to provide information and insight for the future. Yad Vashem's archives and library are among the most important in the world.

The museum itself includes a permanent exhibit that traces the different stages of the Holocaust, beginning with Hitler's rise to power and continuing to the end of World War II.

One of the entrances to the United States Holocaust Memorial Museum.

Yad Vashem also includes several areas that are more memorial in nature than would be the case at a normal museum. There is a Children's Memorial Garden dedicated to the million and a half Jewish children killed by the Nazis. A Valley of the Destroyed Communities lists the names of five thousand places where Jews lived that were destroyed in the Holocaust. Also remembered are the "Righteous Among the Nations," non-Jews like Oskar Schindler, Raoul Wallenberg (see pp. 347–49), and Jan Karski (pp. 163–67), who helped Jews at the risk of their own lives.

An eternal flame burns in the Hall of Remembrance. On the tiled floor are engraved the names of the twenty-two largest concentration and death camps. Ashes from the victims of these camps lie in a vault in front of the eternal flame.

The United States Holocaust Memorial Museum

The United States Holocaust Memorial Museum in Washington, D.C., opened in 1993. The design of the building, including the use of exposed metal and brick, visible fencing and barriers, and boarded windows, evokes a feeling that this is not an ordinary museum, just as the Holocaust was not an ordinary event. Architecture critics were unanimous in praising the success of the design.

Like Yad Vashem, the Holocaust Museum is also a research institution. Its film and photo archives, library, and oral history tapes are available to scholars. In addition, much of the material is computer accessible from the Museum's Learning Center.

Among the items on display are examples of the actual railroad cars used to transport hundreds of thousands of deported Jews to the death camps of Poland.

Anne Frank House

The Anne Frank House in Amsterdam, the Netherlands, is the actual house where Anne and her family hid for twenty-five months. (See Chapter 10, pp. 307–09.) Behind the movable book case are the stairs that lead to the "secret annex" about which Anne wrote. The postcards that Anne used to decorate the walls of her room are still there.

Where to Learn More

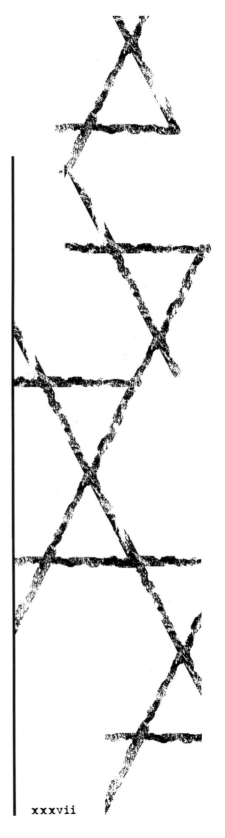

The following list focuses on works written for readers of middle school or high school age. Books aimed at adult readers have been included when they are especially important in providing information or analysis that would otherwise be unavailable, or because they have become classics. All books not specifically written for younger readers are noted as such.

General histories of the Holocaust:

Adler, David A. *We Remember the Holocaust.* New York: Henry Holt, 1995.

Altman, Linda Jacobs. *Forever Outsiders.* Vol. 1 of "Holocaust" series edited by Lisa Clyde Nielsen. Woodbridge, CT: Blackbirch Press, 1998.

Arad, Yithak. *The Pictorial History of the Holocaust.* New York: Macmillan, 1992.

Ayer, Eleanor H. *A Firestorm Unleased.* Vol. 4 of "Holocaust" series, edited by Lisa Clyde Nielsen. Woodbridge, CT: Blackbirch Press, 1998.

Ayer, Eleanor H. *Inferno.* Vol. 5 of "Holocaust" series, edited by Lisa Clyde Nielsen. Woodbridge, CT: Blackbirch Press, 1998.

Ayer, Eleanor H., and Stephen D. Chicoine. *From the Ashes*. Vol. 6 of "Holocaust" series, edited by Lisa Clyde Nielsen. Woodbridge, CT: Blackbirch Press, 1998.

Bachrach, Susan D. *Tell Them We Remember: The Story of the Holocaust*. Boston: Little, Brown, 1994.

Chaikin, Miriam. *A Nightmare in History: The Holocaust, 1933–1945*. New York: Clarion Books, 1987.

Herzstein, Robert E. *The Nazis*. Alexandria, VA: Time-Life Books, 1980.

Meltzer, Milton. *Never to Forget*. New York: Harper & Row, 1976.

Resnick, Abraham. *The Holocaust*. San Diego: Lucent Books, 1991.

Rogasky, Barbara. *Smoke and Ashes*. New York: Holiday House, 1988.

Rossel, Seymour. *The Holocaust: The Fire that Raged*. New York: Franklin Watts, 1989.

Sherrow, Victoria. *The Blaze Engulfs*. Vol. 3 of "Holocaust" series, edited by Lisa Clyde Nielsen. Woodbridge, CT: Blackbirch Press, 1998.

Sherrow, Victoria. *Smoke to Flame*. Vol. 2 of "Holocaust" series, edited by Lisa Clyde Nielsen. Woodbridge, CT: Blackbirch Press, 1998.

Shoenberner, Gerhard. *The Yellow Star: The Persecution of the Jews in Europe, 1933–45*. New York: Bantam Books, 1979.

Shulman, William L., compiler. *Resource Guide*. Vol. 8 of "Holocaust" series, edited by Lisa Clyde Nielsen. Woodbridge, CT: Blackbirch Press. 1998.

Shulman, William L., compiler. *Voices and Visions*. Vol. 7 of "Holocaust" series, edited by Lisa Clyde Nielsen. Woodbridge, CT: Blackbirch Press, 1998.

Strahinich, Helen. *The Holocaust: Understanding and Remembering*. Springfield, NJ: Enslow, 1996.

Wigoder, Geoffrey, ed. *The Holocaust: A Grolier Student Library*. 4 vols. Danbury, CT: Grolier Educational, 1997.

The following general overviews of the Holocaust are aimed at adult readers:

Bauer, Yehuda and Nili Keren. *A History of the Holocaust.* New York: Franklin Watts, 1982.

Dawidowicz, Lucy S. *The War Against the Jews, 1933–1945.* New York: Bantam Books, 1986.

Encyclopedia of the Third Reich. 2 vols. New York: Macmillan, 1991.

Gilbert, Martin. *The Holocaust: The History of the Jews of Europe During the Second World War.* New York: Henry Holt, 1986.

Gutman, Israel, ed. *The Encyclopedia of the Holocaust.* 4 vols. New York: Macmillan, 1990.

Hilberg, Raoul. *The Destruction of the European Jews.* New York: Holmes & Meier, 1985.

Levin, Nora. *The Holocaust: The Nazi Destruction of European Jewry, 1933–1945.* New York: Schocken, 1973.

Snyder, Louis L. *Encyclopedia of the Third Reich.* New York: McGraw-Hill, 1976.

Spiegelman, Art. *Maus: A Survivor's Tale.* Vol. 1, *Maus I: My Father Bleeds History.* New York: Pantheon, 1986. Vol. 2, *Maus II: And Here My Troubles Began.* New York: Pantheon, 1991. *Maus* is written in comic strip form, with the Jews depicted as mice and the Nazis as cats. Despite the format, it is a deadly serious, brilliantly imaginative work. *Maus I* tells the story of Spiegelman's father during the Holocaust; *Maus II* continues his story after the war has ended.

Yahil, Leni. *The Holocaust: The Fate of European Jewry, 1932–1945.* New York: Oxford University Press, 1991.

Zenter, Christian, and Friedemann Bedürftig, eds. *Encyclopedia of the Third Reich.* New York: Da Capo Press 1997.

Atlases:

Gilbert, Martin. *Atlas of the Holocaust.* New York: Macmillan, 1982. Martin, a leading Holocaust scholar, has written this atlas to describe the events of the Holocaust and show where they happened.

United States Holocaust Memorial Museum. *The Historical Atlas of the Holocaust.* New York: Macmillan, 1995. This atlas, also available as a CD-ROM, is aimed at general readers and has quickly become the standard work in the field of Holocaust studies.

German history, the early Nazi movement, the Nazi government, and policy towards the Jews before the Holocaust:

Allen, William Sheridan. *The Nazi Seizure of Power: The Experience of a Single German Town, 1930–1935.* New York: Franklin Watts, 1973. Allen's book is a classic study of the growth of Nazi influence and power. Although it is a work of adult social history, its detailed picture of what the Nazi "revolution" must have felt like to ordinary Germans will reward younger readers who have a strong interest in the subject.

Auerbacher, Inge. *I Am a Star: Child of the Holocaust.* Paramus, NJ: Prentice-Hall, 1986. *I Am a Star* is the memoir of a German Jewish girl who survived Thereisenstadt concentration camp.

Ayer, Eleanor. *Adolf Hitler.* San Diego: Lucent, 1996. Ayer's work describes the life and rise to power of German dictator Adolf Hitler.

Bauer, Yehuda. *Jews for Sale? Nazi-Jewish Negotiations, 1933–1945.* New Haven, CT: Yale University Press, 1994. Bauer's work, written for adults, is about the history of attempts to arrange Jewish emigration, including the role of the Zionist movement.

Berman, Russell A. *Paul von Hindenburg.* New York: Chelsea House, 1987. *Paul von Hindenburg* is a biography of Germany's World War I hero who became president and eventually appointed Hitler as chancellor.

Bosanquest, Mary. *The Life and Death of Dietrich Bonhoeffer.* New York: Harper & Row, 1968. Bosanquest's book describes the role of the Protestant Church during the Holocaust.

Bullock, Alan. *Hitler: A Study in Tyranny.* New York: Harper & Row, 1964. Bullock's biography on Hitler has heavily influenced most other studies.

Crisp, Peter. *The Rise of Fascism.* Charlottesville, VA: Book-wrights, 1991. *The Rise of Fascism* describes fascist movements, including Nazism, through the first half of the twentieth century.

Drucker, Olga Levy. *Kindertransport.* New York: Henry Holt, 1992. *Kindertransport* is the story of German Jewish children who were sent to England in order to escape Nazi persecution.

Eimerl, Sarel. *Hitler Over Europe: The Road to World War II.* Boston: Little, Brown, 1972. Eimerl's book focuses on German foreign policy before the war.

Friedlander, Saul. *Pius XII and the Third Reich.* New York: Knopf, 1966. Although *Pius XII and the Third Reich* is a difficult book for younger readers, it is an important study of the role of the Catholic Church, written by a foremost scholar.

Friedman, Ina R. *Fly Against the Wind: The Story of a Young Woman Who Defied the Nazis.* Bookline, MA: Lodgepole Press, 1995.

Fuller, Barbara. *Germany.* New York: Marshall Cavendish, 1996. Aimed at young readers, *Germany* includes the history, geography, government, and economic background of the country.

Gallo, Max. *The Night of the Long Knives.* New York: Harper & Row, 1972. *The Night of the Long Knives* is an examination of the SA purge and the murder of its leader, Ernst Röhm. Although aimed at an adult audience, it is worth the effort.

Goldston, Robert C. *The Life and Death of Nazi Germany.* New York: Bobbs-Merrill, 1967. Goldston's *The Life and Death of Nazi Germany* includes discussions of the Nazi government and political developments as well as material on foreign affairs.

Graff, Stewart. *The Story of World War II.* New York: E. P. Dutton, 1978.

Halperin, S. William. *Germany Tried Democracy: A Political History of the Reich from 1918 to 1933.* New York: Norton, 1965. Halperin's book was first published in 1946, soon after Germany's defeat in World War II. It remains one of the best works on the history of the Weimar Republic. Aimed at adults, it is detailed and sophisticated, but relatively clear and free from jargon.

Hartenian, Lawrence R. *Benito Mussolini.* New York: Chelsea House, 1988.

Heyes, Eileen. *Adolf Hitler.* Brookfield, CT: Millbrook Press, 1994. Heyes's *Adolf Hitler* provides readers with an insight into the life of Hitler, who rose from obscurity to become the leader of the Nazi Party.

Heyes, Eileen. *Children of the Swastika: The Hitler Youth.* Brookfield, CT: Millbrook Press, 1993. *Children of the Swastika* explores the phenomenon of the Hitler Youth, young people who blindly followed the Nazi policies.

Josephson, Judith P. *Jesse Owens: Track and Field Legend.* Springfield, NJ: Enslow Press, 1997. Josephson's recent biography that does a good job describing the 1936 Berlin Olympics.

Kluger, Ruth Peggy Mann, *Secret Ship.* New York: Doubleday, 1978. *Secret Ship* describes the illegal immigration to Palestine that occurred during the Nazi era.

Leeds, Christopher A. *Italy Under Mussolini.* New York: Wayland, Putnan, 1972. Leeds examines Italian Fascism, which was Hitler's early model for Nazism.

Marrin, Albert. *Hitler.* New York: Viking, 1987. Marrian's book, aimed at young people, focuses on Hitler's personal history and Nazism.

Nevelle, Peter. *Life in the Third Reich: World War II.* North Pomfret, VT: Batsford, 1992. Despite its title, *Life in the Third Reich* is not limited to the war years.

The New Order. Alexandria, VA: Time-Life Books, 1989. *The New Order* depicts Nazi Germany through contemporary photographs.

Niemark, Anne E. *Leo Baeck and the Holocaust.* New York: E.P. Dutton, 1986. Niemark's work is a biography of the leader of the German Jewish community, who eventually was sent to Theresienstadt concentration camp.

Read, Anthony. *Kristallnacht: The Nazi Night of Terror.* New York: Times Books/Random House, 1989. Read's book concentrates on *Kristallnacht,* the night in 1938 when the first public violence broke out against the Jews.

Rubinstein, William D. *The Myth of Rescue.* New York: Routledge, 1997. Rubinstein's book defends American immigration policy during the 1930s. It is a specialized book, aimed at adult readers.

Shirer, William L. *The Rise and Fall of Adolf Hitler.* New York: Random House, 1961. *The Rise and Fall of Adolf Hitler* is a biography aimed at younger readers by Shirer, the American journalist and historian whose *Rise and Fall of the Third Reich* (Simon and Schuster, 1960) is a standard general history for adults.

Skipper, G.C. *Goering and the Luftwaffe.* Danbury, CT: Children's Press, 1980. *Goering and the Luftwaffe* is a biography of Hermann Goering that focuses on his role as leader of the Nazi air force.

Snyder, Louis L. *Hitler's Elite.* New York: Hippocrene Books, 1989. Snyder's book describes the top Nazi leaders. Although it is aimed at general readers, it is not too difficult for young readers.

Snyder, Louis L. *World War II.* New York: Franklin Watts, 1981. Snyder's *World War II* is a military history for young readers.

Speer, Albert. *Inside the Third Reich.* New York: Macmillan, 1970. *Inside the Third Reich* is a fascinating look at the world of the top Nazis. Speer was Hitler's favorite architect, and more importantly, he ran Germany's arms program at the end of the war. The book is aimed at adult readers.

Spence, William. *Germany Then and Now.* New York: Franklin Watts, 1994. Spence's history of Germany is suited for younger readers.

Start, Clarissa. *God's Man: The Story of Pastor Niemöller.* Washburn, 1959. *God's Man* explores the role of former Nazi supporter and Protestant clergyman Martin Niemöller as well as the policies of the Protestant Church during the Nazi era.

Stein, R. Conrad. *Hitler Youth.* Danbury, CT: Children's Press, 1985. Stein's book, aimed at younger readers, discusses the Hitler Youth.

Stewart, Gail. *Hitler's Reich*. San Diego: Lucent Books, 1994. *Hitler's Reich* describes both Hitler's rise to power and what life was like in Nazi Germany.

Thalmann, Rita, and Emmanuel Feinermann. Crystal Night, 9-10 November, 1938. *New York: Putnam, 1974. The decisive turning-point in Nazi policy towards the Jews is described in this work for younger readers.*

Thomas, Gordon, and Max M. Witts. *Voyage of the Damned*. Stein & Day, 1974. *Voyage of the Damned* is about the voyage of the *St. Louis* and, although written for adults, is not too difficult for younger readers.

Toland, John. *Adolf Hitler*. New York: Doubleday, 1976. Although aimed at adult readers, Toland's *Adolf Hitler* contains plenty of valuable information.

Wepman, Dennis. *Adolf Hitler*. New York: Chelsea House, 1989. Wepman's biography includes material on Hitler's methods and rise to power.

Zassenhaus, Hiltgunt. *Walls: Resisting the Third Reich, One Woman's Story*. Boston: Beacon Press, 1974. Zassenhaus's first-person account tells of her attempts as a non-Jewish German woman to oppose the Nazis.

Zurndorfer, Hannele. *The Ninth of November*. Berrien Springs, MI: Quartet Books, 1983. *The Ninth of November* describes *Kristallnacht* from the perspective of one family.

The "Final Solution":

Auschwitz: A History in Photographs. Bloomington: Indiana University Press, 1993. Through photographs, this book tells the history of the death camp.

Breitman, Richard. *The Architect of Genocide: Himmler and the Final Solution*. New York: Knopf, 1991. Breitman's *The Architect of Genocide* describes how Heinrich Himmler, head of the SS, the Nazi military wing, supervised the plan to eliminate the Jews of Europe.

Browning, Christopher R. *Ordinary Men: Reserve Police Battalion 101 and the Final Solution in Poland*. New York: HarperCollins, 1992. *Ordinary Men* includes vivid descriptions of transports to the concentration camps and of shootings by the *Einsatzgruppen*.

Freidlander, Henry. *The Origins of Nazi Genocide*. Chapel Hill: University of North Carolina Press, 1995. *The Origins of Nazi Genocide* is an adult work that examines the euthanasia program.

Friedrich, Otto. *The Kingdom of Auschwitz*. New York: Harper Perennial, 1994. *The Kingdom of Auschwitz* is an adult work, but it is very short and insightful.

Gilbert, Martin. *Auschwitz and the Allies*. New York: Henry Holt, 1990. *Auschwitz and the Allies* is an adult book that gives a balanced opinion of America's policy on saving the Jews.

Goldhagen, Daniel J. *Hitler's Willing Executioners: Ordinary Germans and the Holocaust*. New York: Knopf, 1996. Although especially difficult for young people, *Hitler's Willing Executioners* describes the mass shootings by the *Einsatzgruppen*. Goldhagen's book is at the center of a major controversy about the role and motivation of "ordinary Germans" in Nazi genocide.

Hellman, Peter. *The Auschwitz Album: A Book Based Upon an Album Discovered by a Concentration Camp Survivor, Lili Meier*. New York: Random House, 1981. Hellman's work is a photographic record of the largest of the death camps.

Kogon, Eugen. *The Theory and Practice of Hell: The German Concentration Camps and the System Behind Them*. Los Angeles: Octagon, 1973. Originally written shortly after the war, *The Theory of Practice of Hell* is an adult book that has influenced many later studies.

Leitner, Isabella. *The Big Lie: A True Story*. New York: Scholastic, 1992. *The Big Lie* describes the author's experiences in Auschwitz.

Levi, Primo. *The Drowned and the Saved*. Tempe, AZ: Summit Books, 1988. This is a memoir of the Italian Jewish chemist who survived Auschwitz.

Levi, Primo. *Survival in Auschwitz*. New York: Macmillan, 1987. *Survival in Auschwitz* is Levi's adult work that chronicles his daily activities at the death camp.

Lifton, Robert Jay. *The Nazi Doctors: Medical Killing and the Psychology of Genocide*. New York: Basic Books, 1988. *The Nazi Doctors* is an adult work that discusses the role of the medical profession, including medical experimentation, in the Final Solution.

Millu, Liana. *Smoke Over Birkenau*. Philadelphia: Jewish Publication Society, 1991. *Smoke Over Birkenau* describes the lives of women prisoners at Auschwitz-Birkenau.

Reitlinger, Gerald. *The SS: Alibi of a Nation, 1922–45*. New York: Viking, 1957. Reitlinger's book looks at the SS, the military wing of the Nazi Party

Rubinstein, William D. *The Myth of Rescue*. New York: Routledge, 1997. *The Myth of Rescue* strongly defends Allied war policies, and argues that actions such as bombing Auschwitz were either impossible or useless. This book is probably too specialized for most young readers.

Stein, R. Conrad. *Invasion of Russia*. Danbury, CT: Children's Press, 1985. Despite its title, Stein's work is not limited to military events.

Steiner, Jean Francis. *Treblinka*. New York: Simon & Schuster, 1967. *Treblinka* is an adult work describing the Treblinka uprising.

Stern, Ellen Norman. *Elie Wiesel: Witness for Life*. New York: Ktav Publishing House, 1982. Stern's biography tells of the life of the Nobel Peace Prize-winning author, who survived Auschwitz and Buchenwald as a child.

Weisel, Elie. *The Night Trilogy: Night, Dawn, The Accident*. New York: Hill & Wang 1960, reprinted 1987. *The Night Trilogy* contains three autobiographical books, written for adults, about the Auschwitz and Buchenwald concentration camps.

Willenberg, Samuel. *Surviving Treblinka*. Maldin, MA: Basil Blackwell, 1989. Although *Surviving Treblinka* is aimed at general audiences, the story will also reward younger readers.

Wyman, David S. *The Abandonment of the Jews: America and the Holocaust, 1941–1945*. New York: Pantheon, 1984. Wyman's book is a powerful criticism of American policy toward the issue of saving Jews. It is a specialized book that may be difficult for young readers.

Zyskind, Sara. *Struggle*. Minneapolis, MN: Lerner Publications, 1989. *Struggle* is about Auschwitz.

Poland:

Bernheim, Mark. *Father of the Orphans: The Story of Janusz Korczak*. New York: E.P. Dutton, 1989. *Father of the Orphans* recounts the story of Janusz Korczak, director of the orphanage in the Warsaw ghetto. Korczak and his orphans were deported to the Treblinka death camp, where they were all murdered by the Nazis.

Drucker, Malka, and Michael Halperin. *Jacob's Rescue: A Holocaust Story*. New York: Bantam Skylark, 1993. *Jacob's Rescue* is the story of a Jewish child in Poland.

Gelman, Charles. *Do Not Go Gentle: A Memoir of Jewish Resistance in Poland, 1941–1945*. North Haven, CT: Archon Books, 1989. *Do Not Go Gentle* is the story of a teenage boy who fought as a partisan in Poland.

George, Willy. *In the Warsaw Ghetto, Summer 1941*. New York: Aperture Foundation 1993. *In the Warsaw Ghetto* includes photographs taken secretly by German troops.

Heller, Celia S. *On the Edge of Destruction: Jews of Poland Between the Two World Wars*. New York: Columbia University Press, 1977. Heller's adult work examines Polish Jewish history, sociology, religion, and ideology.

Hyams, Joe. *A Field of Buttercups*. Paramus, NJ: Prentice-Hall, 1968. *A Field of Buttercups* describes the life of Janusz Korczak, the famous Jewish doctor and educator who refused to abandon the children of his Warsaw orphanage.

Keller, Ulrich, ed. *The Warsaw Ghetto in Photographs*. Mineola, NY: Dover, 1984. *The Warsaw Ghetto in Photographs* is based on photographs taken by the Germans in 1941.

Landau, Elaine. *The Warsaw Ghetto Uprising*. New York: Macmillan, 1992. Landau's work concentrates on the story of the rebellion in the Warsaw ghetto.

Sender, Ruth Minsky. *The Cage*. New York: Macmillan, 1986. *The Cage* is an autobiography of Sender, a resident of the Lódz ghetto and a concentration camp survivor.

Sender, Ruth Minsky. *To Life*. New York: Macmillan, 1988. *To Life* picks up where Sender's first autobiography, *The Cage*, leaves off. It describes her liberation at the end of the war, and her search for her family.

Stewart, Gail B. *Life in the Warsaw Ghetto*. San Diego: Lucent Books, 1995. Stewart's book tells the story of the Warsaw ghetto, including the uprising that took place there.

Toll, Nelly S. *Behind the Secret Window: A Memoir of a Hidden Childhood During World War Two*. New York: Dial Books, 1993. *Behind the Secret Window* is the story of a child and her mother hidden by non-Jews in Lwów (Lvov), Poland.

Vishniac, Roman. *A Vanished World*. New York: Farrar, Strauss, & Giroux, 1983. *A Vanished World* uses photographs to describe the world of Poland's Jews before World War II.

Wood, Thomas E. *Karski: How One Man Tried to Stop the Holocaust*. New York: John Wiley, 1994. Wood's adult work discusses some complex political and diplomatic issues, but much of the book is a gripping story about Polish underground officer Jan Karski's attempt to save Poland's Jews.

Ziemian, Joseph. *The Cigarette Seller of Three Crosses Square*. Minneapolis, MN: Lerner Publications, 1975. Ziemian's book describes the life of Jewish children who lived on the "Aryan side" of Warsaw.

Zeinert, Karen. *The Warsaw Ghetto Uprising*. Brookfield, CT: Millbrook Press, 1993.

Other Countries:

Asscher-Pinkoff, Clara. *Star Children*. Detroit: Wayne State University Press, 1986. *Star Children* is the story of children in the Amsterdam ghetto.

Bitton-Jackson, Livia. *I Have Lived a Thousand Years: Growing Up in the Holocaust*. New York: Simon & Schuster, 1997. Bitton-Jackson's memoir discusses her life in Hungary during the Holocaust.

Frank, Anne. *The Diary of Anne Frank*. Edited by Otto Frank. New York: Doubleday, 1952. This first published version of Anne Frank's diary was edited by Frank's father, Otto. He removed some of Frank's criticisms of her mother, who had died at Auschwitz, as well as material that he believed was unsuitable for young people. *The Diary of Anne Frank: The Definitive Edition* (New York: Bantam

Books, 1997) has the sections removed by Otto Frank restored. *The Diary of Anne Frank: The Critical Edition* (New York: Doubleday, 1989) includes additional material about Frank's life before she began writing the diary.

Gies, Miep, and Alison L. Gold. *Anne Frank Remembered.* New York: Simon & Schuster, 1987. *Anne Frank Remembered* is directed at adult readers, but is not too difficult for younger audiences. Gies was the non-Jewish Dutch woman, an employee of Frank's father, who brought the family food in hiding and often spoke with Frank.

Gold, Alison L. *Memories of Anne Frank: Reflections of a Child-hood Friend.* New York: Scholastic, 1997. *Memories of Anne Frank* is the story of Frank's closest friend, called "Hanneli," in Frank's diary.

Handler, Andrew, and Susan Meschel, eds. *Young People Speak.* New York: Franklin Watts, 1993. *Young People Speak* includes eleven authors remembering their childhoods in Hungary during the Holocaust.

Isaacman, Clara. *Clara's Story.* Philadelphia: Jewish Publication Society, 1984. Isaacman's work is the story of a child hiding in the Belgium port city of Antwerp.

Lindwe, Willy. *The Last Seven Months of Anne Frank.* New York: Pantheon, 1991. Lindwe's book describes Frank's time at Bergen-Belsen concentration camp, and is based on the recollections of fellow prisoners who survived.

Perl, Lila, and Marian Blumenthal Lazar. *Four Perfect Pebbles: A Holocaust Story.* New York: Greenwillow Books, 1996. *Four Perfect Pebbles* describes a child who survived the Westerbork transit camp in the Netherlands and then the Bergen-Belsen concentration camp.

Rol, Ruud van der, and Rian Verhoeven. *Anne Frank: Beyond the Diary.* New York: Viking, 1993. *Anne Frank: Beyond the Diary* describes the life of Frank and her family before they went into hiding.

Roth-Hano, Renée. *Touch Wood: A Girlhood in Occupied France.* Portland, OR: Four Winds Press, 1988. Although *Touch Wood* is a nonfiction work, it is written in the style of a novel. The work tells the story of Roth-Hano and her two sisters, who were French Jews hidden in a Catholic convent during Germany's occupation of France.

Siegal, Avanka. *Grace in the Wilderness: After the Liberation, 1945–1948*. New York: Farrar, Strauss, Giroux, 1985. *Grace in the Wilderness* describes Hungarian Jew Siegal's postwar experience.

Siegal, Avanka. *Upon the Head of the Goat: A Childhood in Hungary, 1939–1944*. New York: Farrar, Strauss, Giroux, 1981. Siegal's *Upon the Head of the Goat* is a prize-winning memoir about surviving the Bergen-Belsen concentration camp.

Resistance, survival, rescue, and justice:

Arendt, Hannah. *Eichmann in Jerusalem: A Report on the Banality of Evil*. New York: Penguin, 1977. Arendt's highly controversial work focuses on the "ordinariness" of Adolf Eichmann, the architect of the "Final Solution."

Ayer, Eleanor A. *The United States Holocaust Memorial Museum*. Parsippany, NJ: Silver Burdett Press, 1995. Ayer's book provides a detailed description of the museum and its exhibits.

Bauer, Yehuda. *They Chose Life: Jewish Resistance in The Holocaust*. New York: American Jewish Committee, 1973. Bauer, a major Holocaust scholar, aimed *They Chose Life* at middle-school age readers.

Berenbaum, Michael. *The World Must Know*. Boston: Little, Brown, 1993. *The World Must Know* uses the United States Holocaust Memorial Museum's collection to describe the history of the Holocaust.

Bierman, John. *Righteous Gentile: The Story of Raoul Wallenberg*. New York: Viking, 1981. Bierman's book looks at the life of Wallenberg, a young Swedish diplomat who saved at least 100,000 Hungarian Jews before he disappeared after World War II.

Block, Gay, and Malka Drucker. *Rescuers*. New York: Holmes and Meier, 1992. *Rescuers* includes the stories of four dozen different people, from all over Europe, who hid and saved Jews.

Gilbert, G.M. *Nuremberg Diary*. New York: New American Library, 1947, reprinted New York: Da Capo Press, 1995. *Nuremberg Diary,* originally published soon after the events, was written by Gilbert, the psychologist at the Nuremberg jail during the main trial. The author had complete freedom of access to the defendants and was able to engage in a series of remarkable conversations with them. The book is written for adults and includes some specialized psychological language, but large parts of it provide fascinating and understandable insights into the minds of the top Nazis.

Greenfield, Howard. *The Hidden Children.* New York: Ticknor & Fields, 1993. Greenfield's work describes the experiences of thirteen children hidden by strangers.

Haas, Gerda. *These I Do Remember: Fragments From the Holocaust.* Brooklyn, NY: Cumberland, 1982. *These I Do Remember* consists of excerpts of diaries, letters, and eyewitness accounts of the Holocaust from people all over Europe.

Hausner, Gideon. *Justice in Jerusalem.* New York: Harper & Row, 1966. *Justice in Jerusalem* describes the Adolf Eichmann trial from the viewpoint of the chief prosecutor.

Holliday, Laurel. *Children in the Holocaust and World War II.* New York: Pocket Books, 1995. Holliday's work includes excepts from twenty-two diaries kept by children during the Holocaust, some of whom were killed.

Keneally, Thomas. *Schindler's List.* New York: Simon & Schuster, 1982. Keneally's work, written for adults, is the book on which the award-winning film by Steven Spielberg is based.

Landau, Elaine. *Nazi War Criminals.* New York: Franklin Watts, 1990. *Nazi War Criminals* concerns the escape of wanted Nazis after the war, and the hunt for them.

Landau, Elaine. *We Survived the Holocaust.* New York: Franklin Watts, 1991. *We Survived the Holocaust* includes sixteen stories of survivors.

Linnea, Sharon. *Raoul Wallenberg: The Man Who Stopped Death.* Philadelphia: Jewish Publication Society, 1993. This is a biography of Wallenberg, who saved approximately 100,000 Hungarian Jews from death at the hands of the Nazis.

Meltzer, Milton. *Rescue: The Story of How Gentiles Saved Jews in the Holocaust.* New York: Harper & Row, 1988. Meltzer's book contains chapters on Oskar Schindler and the rescue of the Danish Jews.

Mochizuki, Ken. *Passage to Freedom: The Sugihara Story.* New York: Lee & Low Books, 1997. *Passage to Freedom* is the story of Chiune Sugihara, a Japanese diplomat in Kovno, Lithuania, who defied his government to issue thousands of transit visas to Jews fleeing the Nazis in the summer of 1940.

Morin, Isobel V. *Days of Judgment.* Brookfield, CT: Millbrook Press, 1995. *Days of Judgment* describes the trials of both Nazi and Japanese war criminals after World War II.

Rittner, Carol. *The Courage to Care.* New York: New York University Press, 1986. Rittner's work tells the stories of people who took chances by hiding Jews from the Nazis.

Roberts, Jack L. *Oskar Schindler.* San Diego: Lucent Books, 1996. Robert's biography is of the man who saved tens of thousands of Jews.

Rosenberg, Maxine B. *Hiding to Survive: Stories of Jewish Children Rescued from the Holocaust.* New York: Clarion, 1994. *Hiding to Survive* contains first-person accounts by fourteen Jewish survivors who, as children, were hidden and protected by non-Jews.

Stadtler, Ben. *The Holocaust: A History of Courage and Resistance.* West Orange, NJ: Behrman House, 1974. Stadtler's book discusses the Jewish underground that opposed the Nazis.

Taylor, Teleford. *The Anatomy of the Nuremberg Trials: A Personal Memoir.* New York: Knopf, 1992. Although aimed at adults, *The Anatomy of the Nuremberg Trials* provides a detailed account of the proceedings and the defendants as presented by Taylor, one of the prosecutors at the trials.

Weinberg, Jeshajahu, and Rina Elieli. *The Holocaust Museum in Washington.* New York: Rizzoli, 1995. *The Holocaust Museum in Washington* describes the way the United States Holocaust Memorial Museum was planned and designed to fulfill its purpose.

Fiction Works:

Boraks-Nemetz, Lillian. *The Old Brown Suitcase: A Teenager's Story of War and Peace.* Port Angeles, WA: Ben-Simon Publications, 1994. *The Old Brown Suitcase* tells the story of Slava and her family, who immigrate to Canada from Poland after World War II. As Slava adjusts to her new life, she struggles with her memories of her life in Warsaw before the war, in the ghetto, and in hiding.

Kerr, M. E. *Gentlehands.* New York: HarperCollins, 1978, reprinted Harper Keypoint, 1990. In *Gentlehands,* Buddy Boyle moves in with his grandfather against his parents' wishes, only to discover a terrible secret. Buddy's grandfather was a Nazi official, known as "Gentlehands" by his victims at Auschwitz because he toyed with the emotions of his victims before executing them.

Lowry, Lois. *Number the Stars.* New York: Houghton-Mifflin, 1989. *Number the Stars* is the story of a Danish family who risks their lives by taking in a young Jewish girl and pretending that she is part of their family.

Marvin, Isabel R. *Bridge to Freedom.* Philadelphia: Jewish Publication Society, 1991. *Bridge to Freedom* is the story about Rachel, a young Jewish girl escaping from the Nazis, and Kurt, a fifteen-year-old deserter from the German army. The two become allies as they try to make their way to Belgium and freedom.

Matas, Carol. *Daniel's Story.* New York: Scholastic, 1993. *Daniel's Story* is a fictionalized account based on actual events that children experienced during the Holocaust. It was published in conjunction with "Daniel's Story: Remember the Children," an exhibit at the United States Holocaust Memorial Museum.

Matas, Carol. *Lisa's War.* New York: Scholastic, 1987. *Lisa's War* is the story of thirteen-year-old Lisa, a Jewish girl living in Denmark. After the Germans invade her country and start deporting Jews, Lisa and her bother Stefan become involved in the Resistance.

Orlev, Uri. *The Man From the Other Side.* Translated from the Hebrew by Hillel Halkin. New York: Houghton Mifflin, 1989. In *The Man From the Other Side,* fourteen-year-old Marek, a Catholic, helps to hide a Jewish man from the

Warsaw ghetto. When the uprising occurs, Marek returns to the ghetto with the man to help in the fighting.

Provost, Gary, and Gail Levine-Provost. *David and Max*. Philadelphia: Jewish Publication Society, 1988. *David and Max*, winner of the 1994 National Jewish Book Award, tells the story of David, who spends the summer with his grandfather Max and learns about the horrors of the Holocaust.

Vos, Ida. *Hide and Seek*. Translated by Terese Edelstein and Inez Smidt. New York: Houghton Mifflin, 1981. In *Hide and Seek*, Rachel, a young Jewish girl, tells the story of her family's life in Holland during the German occupation.

Wolff, Virginia Euwer. *The Mozart Season*. New York: Henry Holt, 1991. In *The Mozart Season*, Allegra Shapiro, the youngest competitor in a violin competition, must not only struggle with her music, but also wrestle with her family history as she learns about her great-grandmother, who died in the Treblinka death camp.

Yolen, Jane. *Devil's Arithmetic*. New York: Viking Penguin, 1988. *Devil's Arithmetic* tells the story of Hannah, who is taken back in time during a Passover dinner to her grandfather's village in the 1940s. Soon after she arrives, Hannah and the rest of the Jews of the village are transported to a concentration camp, where every moment is a struggle to survive.

Holocaust Organizations:

There are hundreds of Holocaust organizations throughout the world. We have listed some of the more popular ones here.

ADL Braun Holocaust Institute
823 United Nations Plaza
New York, NY 10017
(212) 885-7804
Web: http://www.adl.org

El Paso Holocaust Museum and Study Center
401 Wallenberg Drive
El Paso, TX 79912
(915) 833-5656
Web: http://www.huntel.com/~hts/holocst.html

Holocaust Education and Memorial Centre of Toronto
4600 Bathurst Street
North York, Ontario
Canada M2R 3V2
(416) 631-5689
Web: http://www.feduja.org

Holocaust Museum Houston
5401 Caroline Street
Houston, TX 77004
(713) 942-8000
Web: http://www.hmh.org

Simon Wiesenthal Center/Museum of Tolerance
9760 West Pico Boulevard
Los Angeles, CA 90035
(310) 553-9036
Web: http://www.wiesenthal.com

Southern Institute for Education and Research
    at Tulane University
Tulane University
MR Box 1692
31 McAlister Drive
New Orleans, LA 70118
(504) 865-6100
Web: http://www.tulane.edu/~so-inst

Tampa Bay Holocaust Memorial Museum
    and Education Center
5001-11th Street
Madeira Beach, FL 33708
(813) 393-4678
Web: http://www.tampabayholocaust.org

United States Holocaust Memorial Museum
100 Raoul Wallenberg Pl., SW
Washington, D.C. 20024
(202) 488-0400
Web: http://www.ushmm.org

Yad Vashem
The Holocaust Martyrs' and Heroes' Remembrance Authority
PO Box 3477
Jerusalem, Israel 91034
972-2-6751611
Web: http://www.yad-vashem.org.il

Picture Credits

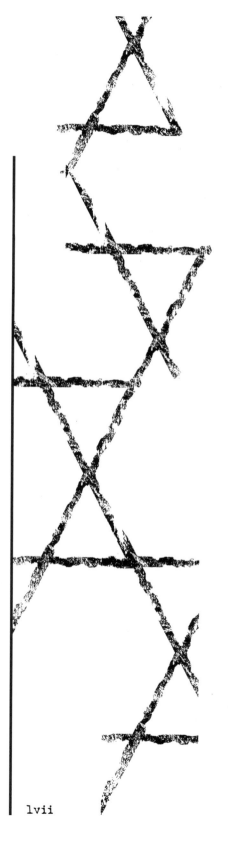

Photographs and illustrations appearing in *Understanding the Holocaust* were received from the following sources:

Cover photo courtesy of the USHMM Photo Archives.

Bildarchiv Preussischer Kulturbesitz. Reproduced by permission: pp. 3, 17, 29, 32, 42, 52, 54, 57, 104, 163, 175, 183, 185, 204, 307, 352, 388; **Foto Marburg/Art Resource. Reproduced by permission:** pp. 13, 15, 49, 101; **AP/Wide World Photos. Reproduced by permission:** pp. 20, 44, 79, 86, 93, 103, 105, 107, 109, 125, 153, 179, 193, 196, 280, 297, 361, 363, 380, 383, 399, 407; **Snark/Art Resource. Reproduced by permission:** pp. 28, 30, 99, 127, 172, 376; **USHMM Photo Archives:** pp. 56, 61, 65, 67, 69, 82, 83, 140, 144, 148, 156, 214, 215, 218, 223, 230, 248, 260, 261, 303, 329, 348, 357, 365, 367, 372, 397; **National Archives/USHMM Photo Archives:** pp. 63, 71, 76, 78, 168, 174, 319, 359, 366; **The Library of Congress/USHMM Photo Archives:** pp. 73, 195; **Photograph by Henry Grossman:** p. 85; **William Gallagher Collection/USHMM Photo Archives. Reproduced by permission:** p. 96; **Stadtarchive Nuerenberg/USHMM Photo Archives. Reproduced**

by permission: p. 112; Lena Fagen/USHMM Photo Archives. Reproduced by permission: p. 118; Trudy Isenberg/USHMM Photo Archives: p. 122; Photograph by Raimund Tisch. USHMM Photo Archives: p. 129; Main Commission for the Investigation of Nazi War Crimes/USHMM Photo Archives. Reproduced by permission: pp. 131, 241, 243, 245, 266, 267, 268; Photograph by Paul Mix. USHMM Photo Archives: p. 133; Rafal Imbro Collection/USHMM Photo Archives. Reproduced by permission: p. 134; YIVO Institute for Jewish Research/USHMM Photo Archives: pp. 137, 270; Amalia Petranker Salsitz Collection/USHMM Photo Archives. Reproduced by permission: p. 151; National Archives in Krakow/USHMM Photo Archives. Reproduced by permission: pp. 159, 215; Irving Milchberg/USHMM Photo Archives: p. 165; Photograph by Heinrich Hoffmann. USHMM Photo Archives: p. 180; State Archives of the Russian Federation/USHMM Photo Archives. Reproduced by permission: p. 187; UPI/Corbis-Bettmann. Reproduced by permission: p. 189; Hessiches Hauptstaatsarchiv/ USHMM Photo Archives. Reproduced by permission: pp. 198, 209; The Library of Congress: pp. 203, 311, 317, 339; Bilderdienst Suddeutscher Verlag. Reproduced by permission: p. 208; Trudi Gidan Collection/USHMM Photo Archives. Reproduced by permission: pp. 217, 227, 304, 337; Photograph by Raimund Tisch. Professor Leopold Pfefferberg-Page Collection/USHMM Photo Archives. Reproduced by permission: p. 221; Photograph by Bernhard Walter. Yad Vashem Photo Archives/USHMM Photo Archives: pp. 225, 235, 252, 344; National Museum in Majdanek/USHMM Photo Archives. Reproduced by permission: p. 232; Photograph by Stanislaw Luczko. Main Commission for the Investigation of Nazi War Crimes/USHMM Photo Archives. Reproduced by permission: p. 249; Archiwum Akt Nowych/USHMM Photo Archives. Reproduced by permission: p. 255; Hadassah Rosensaft Collection/ USHMM Photo Archives. Reproduced by permission: p. 258; State Museum of Auschwitz-Birkenau/USHMM Photo Archives. Reproduced by permission: p. 265; Jerzy Ficowksi/USHMM Photo Archives: p. 272; Yad Vashem Photo Archives/USHMM Photo Archives. Reproduced by permission: p. 276; Central State Archive of Film, Photo and Phonographic Documents/ USHMM Photo Archives. Reproduced by permission: p. 277; Photograph by Fritz

Melbach. USHMM Photo Archives: p. 279; Photograph by William Newhouse. USHMM Photo Archives: p. 281; Government Press Office, Jerusalem/USHMM Photo Archives: p. 286; Frihedsmuseet/ USHMM Photo Archives. Reproduced by permission: p. 292; Toni Heller Collection/ USHMM Photo Archives. Reproduced by permission: p. 295; Henny Kalkstein Reemy Collection/USHMM Photo Archives. Reproduced by permission: p. 306; Photograph by R. Peron. Snark/Art Resource. Reproduced by permission: p. 314; French Embassy Press and Information Division: p. 316; Photograph by Alice Resch-Synnestvedt. USHMM Photo Archives: p. 321; Archive Photos/Popperfoto. Reproduced by Permission: p. 325; Corbis-Bettmann. Reproduced by permission: p. 330; Art Resource. Reproduced by permission: p. 335; Photograph by E.M. Robinson. Alice Lev Collection/USHMM Photo Archives. Reproduced by permission: p. 389; Janina Zimnowodzki/ USHMM Photo Archives: p. 391; Hulton-Getty/The Gamma Liaison Network. Reproduced by permission: p. 378; Archive Photos, Inc. Reproduced by permission: p. 401.

Index

Italic indicates volume numbers;
(ill.) indicates illustrations.

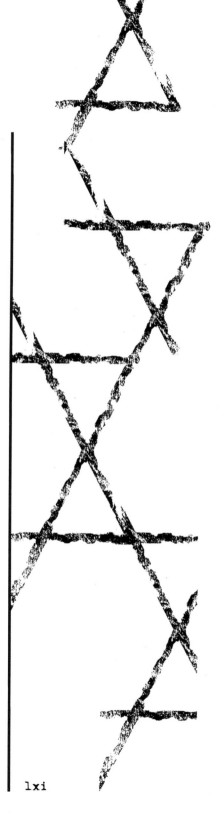